Obsessive-Compulsive Disorder

About the Author

Jonathan S. Abramowitz, PhD, is Associate Professor and director of the OCD/Anxiety Disorders Program at the Mayo Clinic. He has written or edited four books and over 75 research articles and book chapters on OCD and other anxiety disorders. For his contributions to the field, Dr. Abramowitz has received awards from the American Psychological Association and the Mayo Clinic.

Advances in Psychotherapy – Evidence-Based Practice

Danny Wedding; PhD, MPH, Prof., St. Louis, MO
(Series Editor)
Larry Beutler; PhD, Prof., Palo Alto, CA
Kenneth E. Freedland; PhD, Prof., St. Louis, MO
Linda C. Sobell; PhD, ABPP, Prof., Ft. Lauderdale, FL
David A. Wolfe; PhD, Prof., Toronto
(Associate Editors)

The basic objective of this new series is to provide therapists with practical, evidence-based treatment guidance for the most common disorders seen in clinical practice – and to do so in a "reader-friendly" manner. Each book in the series is both a compact "how-to-do" reference on a particular disorder for use by professional clinicians in their daily work, as well as an ideal educational resource for students and for practice-oriented continuing education.

The most important feature of the books is that they are practical and "reader-friendly": All are structured similarly and all provide a compact and easy-to-follow guide to all aspects that are relevant in real-life practice. Tables, boxed clinical "pearls", marginal notes, and summary boxes assist orientation, while checklists provide tools for use in daily practice.

Obsessive-Compulsive Disorder

Jonathan S. Abramowitz
Mayo Clinic, OCD/Anxiety Disorders Program, Rochester, MN

HOGREFE

Library of Congress Cataloging in Publication

is available via the Library of Congress Marc Database under the
LC Control Number 2005936094

Library and Archives Canada Cataloguing in Publication

Abramowitz, Jonathan S
    Obsessive compulsive disorder / Jonathan S. Abramowitz.

(Advances in psychotherapy--evidence-based practice)
Includes bibliographical references.
ISBN 0-88937-316-7

    1. Obsessive-compulsive disorder. 2. Obsessive-compulsive disorder—Treatment.
I. Title. II. Series.

RC533.A27 2005a   616.85›227   C2005-906627-X

© 2006 by Mayo Foundation for Medical Education and Research

PUBLISHING OFFICES
USA: Hogrefe & Huber Publishers, 875 Massachusetts Avenue, 7th Floor,
                 Cambridge, MA 02139
                 Phone (866) 823-4726, Fax (617) 354-6875; E-mail info@hhpub.com
EUROPE: Hogrefe & Huber Publishers, Rohnsweg 25, 37085 Göttingen, Germany
                 Phone +49 551 49609-0, Fax +49 551 49609-88, E-mail hh@hhpub.com

SALES & DISTRIBUTION
USA: Hogrefe & Huber Publishers, Customer Services Department,
                 30 Amberwood Parkway, Ashland, OH 44805
                 Phone (800) 228-3749, Fax (419) 281-6883, E-mail custserv@hhpub.com
EUROPE: Hogrefe & Huber Publishers, Rohnsweg 25, 37085 Göttingen, Germany
                 Phone +49 551 49609-0, Fax +49 551 49609-88, E-mail hh@hhpub.com

OTHER OFFICES
CANADA: Hogrefe & Huber Publishers, 1543 Bayview Avenue, Toronto, Ontario M4G 3B5
SWITZERLAND: Hogrefe & Huber Publishers, Länggass-Strasse 76, CH-3000 Bern 9

Hogrefe & Huber Publishers
Incorporated and registered in the State of Washington, USA, and in Göttingen, Lower Saxony,
Germany

Printed and bound in the USA
ISBN 0-88937-316-7

Preface

This book describes the conceptualization, assessment, and psychological treatment of obsessive-compulsive disorder (OCD) using the empirically supported cognitive-behavioral therapy procedures of **exposure**, **response prevention**, and **cognitive therapy**. The development of effective problem-focused treatments for psychological disorders such as OCD has created an enormous need for the dissemination of treatment programs, such as this one, to mental health professionals who want to know how to use such techniques with their patients. This book builds upon psychological principles of behavior change. As such, it assumes basic knowledge and some training in psycho-therapeutic intervention. It is written for psychologists, psychiatrists, social workers, students and trainees, and other mental health care practitioners. It is intended not only for those specializing in OCD or other anxiety disorders, but for those clinicians who wish to learn how to manage OCD effectively in their day-to-day practice.

The book is divided into five chapters. The first chapter describes the clinical phenomenon of OCD, differentiating it from other disorders with similar characteristics and outlining empirically supported diagnostic and assessment procedures. Chapter 2 reviews what is known about the leading theoretical models of the development and maintenance of OCD, and their treatment implications. In Chapter 3, I present a framework for conducting an initial assessment and for deciding whether a particular patient is a candidate for the psychological treatment program outlined in Chapter 4. Methods for explaining the diagnosis of OCD and introducing the treatment program are incorporated. Chapter 4 presents in detailed fashion the nuts and bolts of effective psychological treatment techniques for OCD. There are numerous case examples and transcripts of in-session dialogs to illustrate the treatment procedures. The chapter also reviews scientific evidence for the efficacy of this program, and describes a number of common obstacles to successful treatment. Finally, Chapter 5 includes a series of case examples describing the treatment of various sorts of OCD symptoms (contamination, fears of responsibility for harm, etc.). A variety of forms and patient handouts for use in treatment appear in the book's Appendix.

OCD is a highly heterogeneous disorder. For example, some patients experience fears of germs and contamination, while others have recurring unwanted anxiety-evoking ideas of committing heinous acts that they are unlikely to commit (e.g., running into pedestrians while driving, murdering loved ones). It is rare to see two sufferers with completely overlapping symptoms. Although a systematic and multicomponent treatment approach is advocated in this book, this manual is not intended as a cookbook. Instead, the clinician is guided in tailoring specific treatment components to individual patients' needs. This manual provides a practical and structured approach with supporting didactic materials for both clinicians and patients.

Acknowledgments

I am indebted to a large group of people, including series editor Danny Wedding and Robert Dimbleby of Hogrefe and Huber, for their invaluable guidance and suggestions. The pages of this book echo with clinical wisdom I acquired during my pre- and postdoctoral training at the Center for Treatment and Study of Anxiety in Philadelphia, where I spent many hours learning about OCD and its treatment from master clinicians such as Martin Franklin and Michael Kozak, who also took a genuine interest in my professional development. In addition, I wish to thank my undergraduate and graduate academic mentors—Kathleen Harring, T. Joel Wade, and Art Houts—for impressing upon me the importance of science in psychology and psychological practice.

I am also grateful for the support of my wonderful colleagues at Mayo Clinic, including Stephen Whiteside, Sarah Kalsy, Brett Deacon (now at the University of Wyoming), Katherine Moore, Stefanie Schwartz (now in private practice in Florida), Kristi Dahlman, and Jill Snuggerud. I owe a great deal to my remarkably competent secretary, Marcia Redalen, who oversees my daily schedule and frequently communicates with patients.

This book is dedicated to all of the patients and research participants who have come to our clinic seeking help and, not knowing what to expect of treatment, found the courage to confront their fears and defeat their anxiety. They believed in us, confided in us, challenged us, and educated us.

Most of all, this book would not be possible without the enduring love, support, and patience of my wife Stacy, and our children, Emily and Miriam. Their affection inspires me to do my very best every day. With their help, I have gained a clearer sense of who I am as a person, a father, a husband, and a psychologist.

Dedication

To my parents, Ferne and Les Abramowitz—*my only creators*

Table of Contents

1

Description

1.1 Terminology

Obsessive-compulsive disorder (OCD) (300.3) was previously known as obsessive-compulsive neurosis. It is sometimes considered part of a spectrum of conditions characterized by more or less similar features (see Section 1.5).

1.2 Definition

OCD is classified in the DSM-IV-TR (American Psychiatric Association, 2000) as an anxiety disorder (300.3) defined by the presence of **obsessions** or **compulsions** (see Table 1). Obsessions are persistent intrusive thoughts, ideas, images, impulses, or doubts that are experienced as unacceptable, senseless, or bizarre and that evoke subjective distress in the form of anxiety or doubt.

Definition of obsessions and compulsions

Table 1
DSM-IV Diagnostic Criteria for OCD

A. Either obsessions or compulsions.

Obsessions are defined by (1), (2), (3), and (4):

(1) repetitive and persistent thoughts, images, or impulses that are experienced, at some point, as intrusive and inappropriate and that cause marked anxiety or distress
(2) the thoughts, images, or impulses are not worries about real-life problems
(3) the person tries to ignore or suppress the thoughts, images, or impulses, or neutralize them with some other thought or action
(4) the thoughts, images, or impulses are recognized as a product of one's own mind and not imposed from without

Compulsions are defined as (1) and (2):

(1) repetitive behaviors or mental acts that one feels driven to perform in response to an obsession or according to certain rules
(2) the behaviors or mental acts are aimed at preventing or reducing distress or preventing feared consequences; however the behaviors or mental acts are clearly excessive or are not connected in a realistic way with what they are designed to neutralize or prevent

B. At some point during the disorder the person has recognized that the obsessions or compulsions are excessive or unreasonable.

DSM-IV diagnostic
criteria for OCD

Table 1
continued

C. The obsessions or compulsions cause marked distress, are time-consuming (take more than 1 hour a day), or significantly interfere with usual daily functioning.

D. The content of the obsessions or compulsions is not better accounted for by another Axis I disorder, if present. (e.g., concern with appearance in the presence of body dysmorphic disorder, or preoccupation with having a serious illness in the presence of hypochondriasis).

E. Symptoms are not due to the direct physiological effects of a substance or a general medical condition.

Specify if:

With poor insight: if for most of the time the person does not recognize that their obsessions and compulsions are excessive or unreasonable.

Adapted from the DSM-IV diagnostic criteria for OCD (American Psychiatric Association, 1994, pp. 422–423). Adapted with permission.

Although highly specific to the individual, obsessions typically concern the following themes: aggression and violence, responsibility for causing harm (e.g., by mistakes), contamination, sex, religion, the need for exactness or completeness, and serious illnesses (e.g., cancer). Most patients with OCD evidence multiple types of obsessions. Examples of common and uncommon obsessions appear in Table 2.

Compulsions are urges to perform behavioral or mental rituals to reduce the anxiety or the probability of harm associated with obsessions. Compulsive rituals are deliberate, yet clearly senseless or excessive in relation to the obsessional fear they are designed to neutralize. As with obsessions, rituals are

Examples of common
and uncommon
obsessions

Table 2
Common and Uncommon Obsessions

Common obsessions

 – Thoughts of contamination from germs, dirt, fungus, animals, body waste, or household chemicals
 – Persistent fears and doubts that one is (or may become) responsible for harm or misfortunes such as fires, burglaries, awful mistakes, injuries
 – Unacceptable sexual ideas (e.g., molestation)
 – Unwanted violent impulses (e.g., to attack a helpless person)
 – Unwanted sacrilegious thoughts (e.g., desecrating a synagogue)
 – Need for order, symmetry, completeness
 – Fears of certain numbers (e.g., 13, 666), colors (e.g., red), or words (e.g., murder)

Uncommon obsessions

 – Fear of having an extramarital affair with a stranger by mistake
 – Fear of becoming someone else
 – Fear of absorbing calories by touching food
 – Fear of contamination from a geographic region

Table 3 **Common and Uncommon Compulsive Rituals**	Examples of common and uncommon compulsions

Common rituals

- Washing one's hands 50 times per day or taking multiple (lengthy) showers
- Repeatedly cleaning objects or vacuuming the floor
- Returning several times to check that the door is locked
- Placing items in the "correct" order to achieve "balance"
- Re-tracing one's steps
- Re-reading or re-writing things to prevent mistakes
- Calling relatives or "experts" to ask for reassurance
- Thinking the word "life" to counteract hearing the word "death"
- Repeated and excessive confessing of one's "sins"
- Repeating a prayer until it is said perfectly

Uncommon rituals

- Repeating oneself to ensure that others understand what has been said
- Having to look at certain points in space in a specified way
- Having to mentally rearrange letters in sentences to spell out comforting words

highly patient-specific. Examples of behavioral (overt) rituals include repetitious hand washing, checking (e.g., locks, the stove), counting, and repeating routine actions (e.g., going through doorways). Examples of mental rituals include excessive prayer and using special phrases or numbers to neutralize obsessional fear. Table 3 presents examples of some common and uncommon compulsive rituals.

1.2.1 Insight

Patients with OCD show a range of "insight" into the senselessness of their obsessions and compulsions—some acknowledge the irrationality of their symptoms while others are firmly convinced (approaching delusional intensity) that the symptoms are rational. To accommodate this parameter of the clinical picture of OCD, the diagnostic specifier "with poor insight" is used to indicate that the patient believes his or her fears and rituals are reasonable. Often, the degree of insight varies across time and obsessional themes. For example, a patient might recognize his or her contamination fears as senseless, yet have poor insight into the irrationality of a fear of causing harm to others.

Patients vary in terms of their insight into the senseless of their symptoms

1.3 Epidemiology

OCD has a one-month prevalence of 1.3% and a lifetime prevalence of 2-3% in the adult population (this is equivalent to 1 in 40 adults) (Karno, Golding, Sorenson, & Burnam, 1988). The disorder affects men and women in equal numbers, although among children, boys have a higher prevalence rate than girls.

Despite its relatively high prevalence (OCD is the 4th most common psychological disorder after depression, substance abuse, and phobias), most individuals with OCD suffer for several years before they receive adequate diagnosis and treatment. Factors contributing to the under-recognition of OCD include the failure of patients to disclose symptoms, the failure to screen for obsessions and compulsions during mental status examinations, and difficulties with differential diagnoses (see Section 1.5).

1.4   Course and Prognosis

OCD generally runs a chronic and deteriorating course

OCD symptoms typically develop gradually. An exception is the abrupt onset sometimes observed following pregnancy. The modal age of onset is 6-15 years in males and 20-29 years in females. Generally, OCD has a low rate of spontaneous remission. Left untreated, the disorder runs a chronic and deteriorating course, although symptoms may wax and wane in severity over time (often dependent upon levels of psychosocial stress).

1.5   Differential Diagnoses

OCD is often confused with other disorders with similar features

In clinical practice, OCD can be difficult to differentiate from a number of disorders with deceptively similar symptom patterns. Moreover, the terms "obsessive" and "compulsive" are often used indiscriminately to refer to phenomena that are not clinical obsessions and compulsions as defined by the DSM-IV-TR. This section highlights key differences between the symptoms of OCD and those of several other disorders.

1.5.1   Generalized Anxiety Disorder (GAD)

Anxious apprehension may be present in both OCD and GAD. However, whereas worries in GAD concern real-life problems (e.g., finances, relationships), obsessions in OCD contain senseless or bizarre content that is not about general life problems (e.g., fear of contracting AIDS from walking into a hospital). Moreover, the content of worries in GAD may shift frequently, whereas the content of obsessional fears is generally stable over time.

1.5.2   Depression

OCD and depression both involve repetitive negative thoughts. However, depressive ruminations are generalized, pessimistic ideas about the self, world, or future (e.g., "no one likes me") with frequent shifts in content. Unlike obsessions, ruminations are not strongly resisted and they do not elicit avoidance or compulsive rituals. Obsessions can be thoughts, ideas, images, and impulses that involve fears of specific disastrous consequences with infrequent shifts in content.

1.5.3   Tics and Tourette's Syndrome (TS)

Both OCD and TS sometimes involve stereotyped or rapid movements. However, tics (as in TS) are spontaneous acts evoked by a sensory urge. They serve to reduce sensory tension rather than as an escape from obsessive fear. In contrast, compulsions in OCD are deliberate acts evoked by affective distress and the urge to reduce fear.

1.5.4   Delusional Disorders (e.g., Schizophrenia)

Both OCD and delusional disorders involve bizarre, senseless, and fixed thoughts and beliefs. These thoughts might evoke affective distress in both conditions. However, unlike obsessions, delusions do not lead to compulsive rituals. Schizophrenia is also accompanied by other negative symptoms of thought disorders (e.g., loosening associations) that are not present in OCD.

1.5.5   Impulse Control Disorders

Excessive and repetitive behaviors might be present in both OCD and impulse control disorders such as pathological gambling, pathological shopping/buying, trichotillomania, kleptomania, compulsive internet use (e.g., viewing pornography) and "sexual compulsions." For this reason, impulse control disorders are sometimes considered part of an "OCD spectrum." However, the repetitive behaviors in impulse control disorders are performed to achieve a thrill or rush (i.e., they are **impulsive**), whereas **compulsive** rituals in OCD are performed to escape from distress. Although individuals with impulse control disorders may experience guilt, shame, and anxiety associated with their problematic behaviors, their anxiety is not triggered by obsessional cues as in OCD. Obsessions are not present in impulse control disorders.

1.5.6   Obsessive Compulsive Personality Disorder (OCPD)

Whereas OCD and OCPD have overlapping names, there are more differences than similarities between the two conditions. OCPD is a set of pervasive traits that involve rigidity and inflexibility, meticulousness, and sometimes impulsive anger and hostility. People with OCPD view these traits as functional and therefore consistent with their world view (i.e., they are "ego-syntonic"). On the other hand, OCD symptoms are experienced as upsetting and incongruent with the person's world view (i.e., "ego-dystonic"). Hence, OCD symptoms are resisted, whereas OCPD symptoms are not.

1.5.7   Hypochondriasis

Persistent thoughts about illnesses and repetitive checking for reassurance can be present in both OCD and hypochondriasis (sometimes considered an OCD spectrum disorder). In OCD, however, patients evidence additional obsessive themes (e.g., aggression, contamination), whereas in hypochondriasis, patients are singly obsessed with their health.

1.5.8   Body Dysmorphic Disorder (BDD)

Both BDD (also considered part of an OCD spectrum) and OCD can involve intrusive, distressing thoughts concerning one's appearance. Moreover, repeated checking might be observed in both disorders. However, whereas people with OCD also have other obsessions, the focus of BDD symptoms is limited to one's appearance.

1.6   Comorbidities

Comorbidity is common in OCD

Comorbidity with other Axis I disorders is more common in OCD than in other anxiety disorders. The most frequently co-occurring diagnoses are depressive disorders and other anxiety disorders. About 50% of people with OCD have experienced at least one major depressive episode (or dysthymia) in their lives. Commonly co-occurring anxiety disorders include generalized anxiety disorder, panic disorder, and social phobia, with rates ranging from 30% to 45% (Crino & Andrews, 1996a). When comorbid depression is present, OCD typically predates the depressive symptoms, suggesting that depressive symptoms usually occur in response to the distress and functional impairment associated with OCD (rather than as a precursor). Depressive symptoms also seem to be more strongly related to the severity of obsessions than to compulsions. Less frequently, individuals with OCD have comorbid eating disorders, tic disorders (e.g., Tourette's syndrome), and impulse control disorders.

Axis II (personality) disorders may also co-occur with OCD, although available prevalence rates have ranged widely (from 8.7% to 87.5%) depending on how the Axis II psychopathology is assessed. Studies generally agree that personality disorders belonging to the anxious cluster (e.g., obsessive-compulsive, avoidant) are more common than those of other clusters (Crino & Andrews, 1996b).

1.7   Diagnostic Procedures and Documentation

This section reviews the empirically established structured and semi-structured diagnostic interviews and self-report measures for assessing the presence and severity of OCD symptoms, as well as for documenting changes in these symptoms during a course of psychological treatment.

1.7.1 Structured Diagnostic Interviews

Two structured diagnostic interviews that are based on DSM-IV-TR criteria can be used to confirm the diagnosis of OCD and common comorbid disorders: the **Anxiety Disorders Interview Schedule for DSM-IV** (ADIS-IV; Di Nardo, Brown, & Barlow, 1994) and the **Structured Clinical Interview for DSM-IV** (SCID-IV; First, Spitzer, Gibbon, & Williams, 2002). Both of these instruments possess good reliability and validity. The SCID is available over the Internet at www.scid4.org, and the ADIS is available from Oxford University Press.

1.7.2 Semi-Structured Symptom Interviews

OCD is unique among the emotional disorders in that the form and content of its symptoms can vary widely from one patient to the next. In fact, two individuals with OCD might present with completely nonoverlapping symptoms. Such heterogeneity necessitates a thorough assessment of the **topography** of the patient's symptoms: what types of obsessions and compulsions are present and how severe are these symptoms?

Yale-Brown Obsessive Compulsive Scale (Y-BOCS)

The Y-BOCS (Goodman, Price, Rasmussen, Mazure, Delgado et al., 1989; Goodman, Price, Rasmussen, Mazure, Fleischmann et al., 1989), which includes a symptom checklist and a severity rating scale, is ideal for addressing these questions. From 30–60 minutes might be required to administer this semi-structured interview. A full copy of the measure appears in the *Journal of Clinical Psychiatry*, volume 60 (1999), supplement 18, pages 67–77. The first part of the Y-BOCS Symptom Checklist provides definitions and examples of obsessions and compulsions that the clinician reads to the patient. Next, the clinician reviews a list of over 50 common obsessions and compulsions and asks the patient whether each symptom is currently present or has occurred in the past. Finally, the most prominent obsessions, compulsions, and OCD-related avoidance behaviors are listed.

The Y-BOCS—a measure of OCD symptom severity

There have been no psychometric studies of the Y-BOCS Checklist, yet clinical observation suggests that the instrument is quite comprehensive. One limitation is that it assesses obsessions and compulsions according to **form** rather than **function**. It is therefore up to the clinician to inquire about the relationship between obsessions and compulsions (i.e., which obsessional thoughts evoke which rituals). A second limitation is that the checklist contains only one item assessing mental rituals. Thus, the clinician must probe in a less structured way for the presence of these covert symptoms. The assessment of mental rituals is discussed further in Section 4.1.1.

The Y-BOCS Severity Scale includes 10 items to assess the following five parameters of obsessions (items 1–5) and compulsions (items 6–10): (a) time, (b) interference, (c) distress, (d) efforts to resist, and (e) perceived control. Each item is rated on a scale from 0 to 4 and the item scores are summed to produce a total score ranging from 0 (no symptoms) to 40 (extreme). Table 4 shows the clinical breakdown of scores on the Y-BOCS severity scale. The measure has acceptable reliability, validity, and sensitivity to change. An advantage of the

Table 4
Clinical Breakdown of Scores on the Y-BOCS Severity Scale

Y-BOCS score	Clinical severity
0–7	Subclinical
8–15	Mild
16–23	Moderate
24–31	Severe
32–40	Extreme

Y-BOCS is that it assesses OCD symptom severity independent of symptom content. However, a drawback of this approach is that the clinician must be cautious to avoid rating the symptoms of other disorders (e.g., GAD, impulse control disorders) as obsessions or compulsions.

Brown Assessment of Beliefs Scale (BABS)

The BABS—a measure of insight in OCD

Since poor insight has been linked to attenuated treatment outcome, initial assessment of OCD should include determination of the extent to which the patient perceives his or her obsessions and compulsions as senselessness and excessive. The BABS (Eisen et al., 1998) is a semi-structured interview that contains 7 items and assesses insight as a continuous variable. The patient first identifies one or two current obsessional fears (e.g., "If I touch dirty laundry without washing my hands, I will become sick"). Next, individual items assess (a) conviction in this belief, (b) perceptions of how others view this belief, (c) explanation for why others hold a different view, (d) willingness to challenge the belief, (e) attempts to disprove the belief, (f) insight into the senselessness of the belief, and (g) ideas/delusions of reference. Each item is rated on a scale from 0 to 4 and the first six items are summed to obtain a total score of 0 to 24 (higher scores indicate poorer insight). The seventh item is not included in the total score. The BABS has good reliability, validity, and sensitivity to change. It is available from Dr. Jane Eisen at Brown University School of Medicine.

Hamilton Rating Scale for Depression (HRSD)

Because the majority of individuals with OCD also experience depressive symptoms, the assessment of mood complaints via a semi-structured interview is recommended. The HRSD (Hamilton, 1960) is a well-studied tool that measures cognitive (e.g., feelings of guilt), affective (e.g., current mood state), and somatic (e.g., appetite, sleep) aspects of depression. The scale has adequate psychometric properties and is also sensitive to the effects of treatment. It is available on the internet at: http://www.strokecenter.org/trials/scales/hamilton.pdf.

1.7.3   Self-Report Inventories

Self-report inventories are used to gather additional severity data

Psychometrically validated self-report questionnaires can be used to supplement the clinical interviews described above. Such questionnaires are easily administered, carefully worded, and have well-established norms. Accordingly, they are best used to corroborate information obtained from clinical interviewing and to monitor symptom severity during treatment.

Obsessive Compulsive Inventory—Revised (OCI-R)

The OCI-R (Foa, Huppert, Leiberg, Langner, Kichic, Hajcak, & Salkovskis, 2002) consists of 18 items that measure a wide range of obsessive-compulsive symptoms. Each item (e.g., "I check things more often than necessary") is rated on a 5-point scale of distress associated with that particular symptom. The OCI-R has six subscales corresponding to various presentations of OCD: washing, checking, ordering, obsessing, hoarding, and neutralizing. Each subscale contains three items which are summed to produce subscale scores (range = 0–12). A total score (range = 0–72) may be calculated by summing all 18 items. The OCI-R, which is psychometrically sound, is printed in the journal *Psychological Assessment*, volume 14 (2002), on page 496.

The OCI-R—a brief measure of OCD severity

Beck Depression Inventory (BDI)

The BDI (Beck, Ward, Medelsohn, Mock, & Erlbaugh, 1961) is one of the most widely used self-report measures of depression. It contains 21-items that assess the cognitive, affective, and somatic features of global distress. The BDI has good psychometric properties and is easy to administer and score. Patients typically need from 5 to 10 minutes to complete the scale and scores of 20 or greater usually indicate the presence of clinical depression. The BDI is available from the Psychological Corporation.

Beck Anxiety Inventory (BAI)

The BAI (Beck, Epstein, Brown & Steer, 1988) is a reliable, valid, and widely used measure of general anxiety. It consists of 21 items that assess the cognitive, physiological, and behavioral components of anxiety. The BAI is also available from the Psychological Corporation.

1.7.4   Documenting Changes in Symptom Levels

Continual assessment of OCD and related symptoms throughout the course of psychological treatment assists the clinician in evaluating treatment response. It is not enough to simply assume that "he seems to be less obsessed," or "it looks like she has cut down on her compulsions," or even for the patient to report that he or she now "feels better." Periodic assessment and comparison with baseline symptom levels using psychometrically validated self-report and interview measures should be conducted to clarify objectively in what ways treatment has been helpful and what work remains to be done.

Assessing OCD symptoms throughout treatment

2

Theories and Models

A number of theories have been proposed to explain the development and clinical picture of OCD. This chapter reviews several theoretical models that have been well-studied, with an emphasis on the cognitive-behavioral model which forms the basis of the treatment program described in Chapter 4.

2.1 Neuropsychiatric Theories

2.1.1 Neurochemical Theories

Neuropsychiatric theories of OCD

Neuropsychiatric theories of OCD can be categorized into neurochemical theories and neuroanatomical theories. Prevailing neurochemical theories posit that abnormalities in the serotonin system, particularly the hypersensitivity of postsynaptic serotonergic receptors, underlie OCD symptoms (Gross, Sasson, Chorpa, & Zohar, 1998). This "serotonin hypothesis" was proposed following observations that serotonergic medication, but not other kinds of antidepressants, were effective in reducing OCD symptoms. However, results from numerous studies that have directly examined the relationship between serotonin and OCD have been inconsistent. For instance, some studies report increased concentrations of serotonin metabolites in the cerebrospinal fluid of OCD patients relative to nonpatients; other studies do not report such findings. Whereas the preferential response of OCD to serotonergic medication is often championed as supporting the serotonin hypothesis, this argument is of little value since the hypothesis was derived from this treatment outcome result. Thus, whether serotonin functioning mediates OCD symptoms remains unclear.

2.1.2 Neuroanatomical Theories

Predominant neuroanatomical models of OCD propose that obsessions and compulsions arise from structural and functional abnormalities in particular areas of the brain, specifically the orbitofrontal-subcortical circuits (Saxena, Bota, & Brody, 2001). These circuits are thought to connect regions of the brain involved in processing information with those involved in the initiation of certain behavioral responses; and their overactivity is thought to lead to OCD. Neuroanatomic models have been derived from imaging studies in which activity levels in specific brain areas are compared between OCD patients and healthy controls. For example, positron emission tomography (PET) studies have consistently found increased glucose utilization in the orbitofrontal cortex (OFC) among patients with OCD as compared to nonpatients.

Although highly interesting, neuroanatomical studies are cross-sectional and therefore do not reveal whether OCD is caused by apparent dysfunctions in the brain. It is possible that the observed alterations in brain function represent normally functioning brain systems that are affected by having a chronic anxiety disorder such as OCD.

2.2 Psychological Theories

2.2.1 Learning Theory

The learning (conditioning) model of OCD is based on the two-factor theory of fear which proposes that obsessional anxiety is acquired by classical conditioning and maintained by operant conditioning (Mowrer, 1960). For example, the obsessional fear of floors is said to arise from a traumatic experience during which anxiety becomes associated with floors. This fear is then maintained by behaviors that prevent the natural extinction of the fear, such as avoidance of floors and compulsive washing after contact with the floor. Avoidance and rituals are also negatively reinforced by the immediate (albeit temporary) reduction in discomfort that they engender.

A learning (conditioning) model

Research supports some aspects of the learning theory. For example, obsessional stimuli (thoughts, ideas, images, and associated stimuli) **evoke** anxiety, and compulsive rituals bring about an immediate **reduction** in anxiety and distress (Rachman, 1980). However, other features are unsupported. For instance, obsessions do not appear to develop through classical conditioning (e.g., from traumatic experiences). Thus, the learning model provides a basis for understanding the persistence of OCD symptoms, particularly rituals, but does not adequately account for the development of obsessional fear.

2.2.2 Cognitive Deficit Models

Compared to nonpatients, people with OCD evidence abnormalities on a range of cognitive tasks such as executive functioning, cognitive inhibition, and some forms of memory. However, these deficits are not found in all patients, and even when they are present, they tend to be mild. Nevertheless, some theorists have suggested that OCD arises from aberrations in general information processing systems. The deficits are general in the sense that they affect both neutral and OCD-related information (McNally, 2000).

Cognitive deficit models

Cognitive deficit models have two key limitations. First, they do not account for the heterogeneity of OCD symptoms (e.g., why some patients have contamination obsessions while others have sexual obsessions). Second, because mild cognitive deficits are present in many disorders (e.g., panic, bulimia nervosa) these models fail to explain why such deficits give rise to OCD instead of one of these other disorders. Thus, if cognitive deficits play a causal role in OCD, they most likely represent a nonspecific vulnerability factor that might (or might not) contribute to the etiology of obsessions and compulsions.

2.2.3   Contemporary Cognitive-Behavioral Models

Contemporary cognitive-behavioral models of OCD form the basis for CBT

The treatment program described in this book is based on a cognitive-behavioral approach in which OCD is thought to arise from specific sorts of dysfunctional beliefs (Shafran, 2005). Cognitive-behavioral models begin with the well-established finding that intrusive thoughts (i.e., thoughts, images, and impulses that intrude into consciousness) are normal experiences that most people have from time to time. Sometimes triggered by external stimuli (e.g., thoughts of a house fire that are triggered by the sight of a fire truck), such intrusions usually reflect the person's current concerns. Research also shows that people with no history of OCD have intrusive thoughts about "taboo" topics such as sex, violence, blasphemy, and germs.

The model proposes that normal intrusions develop into highly distressing and time-consuming clinical obsessions when the intrusions are mistakenly appraised as posing a threat for which the individual is personally responsible. For example, consider the unwanted impulse to yell a curse word in a quiet place such as a church or a theatre. Most people would consider such an intrusive impulse as meaningless and harmless (e.g., "mental noise"). However, according to the cognitive-behavioral model, such an intrusion would develop into a clinical obsession if the person attaches to it a high degree of importance, leading to an escalation in negative emotion—for example, "Thinking about yelling in church means I'm an immoral person," or "I must be extra careful to make sure I don't lose control." Such appraisals evoke distress and motivate the person to try to suppress or neutralize the unwanted thought (e.g., by praying or replacing it with a "safe" thought), and to attempt to prevent any harmful events associated with the intrusion (e.g., by avoiding churches).

Compulsive rituals are conceptualized as maladaptive efforts to remove intrusions and to prevent feared consequences. However, there are several ways in which rituals are counterproductive. First, they are technically "effective" in temporarily providing the desired reduction in obsessional distress. Therefore, these strategies are negatively reinforced, and frequently evolve into behavioral patterns that consume substantial time and effort (i.e., they become "compulsive") and impair the individual's ability to function. Second, because they reduce anxiety in the short term, rituals prevent the natural abatement of the fear response that typically occurs when individuals stay in feared situations for longer periods of time. Third, rituals lead to an increase in the frequency of obsessions by serving as reminders of obsessional intrusions, thereby triggering their reoccurrence. For example, compulsively checking the stove can trigger intrusions about house fires. Attempts at distracting oneself from unwanted intrusions may paradoxically increase the frequency of intrusions, possibly because the distractors become reminders (retrieval cues) of the intrusions. Finally, performing rituals preserves dysfunctional beliefs and misinterpretations of obsessional

Table 5
Summary of Maintenance Processes in OCD

Maintenance process	Description
Selective attention	Hypervigilance for threat cues enhances the detection of obsessional stimuli.
Physiological factors	The fight-or-flight response is a normal response to perceived threat. Emotional reasoning reaffirms mistaken beliefs that lead to feeling anxious.
Safety-seeking behavior	Overt and covert rituals, reassurance-seeking, and neutralizing strategies are reinforced by the immediate reduction in distress they engender. In the long-term, these strategies prevent disconfirmation of mistaken beliefs because of how their outcomes are incorrectly interpreted.
Passive avoidance	Avoidance produces temporary anxiety reduction, but prevents disconformation of overestimates of risk because the person never has the opportunity to find out that danger is unlikely.
Concealment of obsessions	Hiding obsessions from others prevents disconfirmation of mistaken beliefs about the normalcy of intrusive thoughts.
Attempted thought control	Attempts to control or suppress unwanted thoughts lead to an increase in unwanted thoughts. Misappraisal of thought control failure leads to further distress.

thoughts. That is, when feared consequences do not occur after performance of a ritual, the person attributes this to the ritual that was performed.

To summarize, when a person appraises an otherwise normally occurring mental intrusion as posing a threat for which he or she is responsible, the person becomes distressed and attempts to remove the intrusion and prevent the feared consequences. This paradoxically increases the frequency of intrusions. Thus, the intrusions escalate into persistent and distressing clinical obsessions. Because the obsessional thought is experienced as distressing, it evokes urges to perform some response—overt or covert—to neutralize the distress and reduce the probability of a feared outcome. Compulsions maintain the intrusions and prevent the self-correction of mistaken (catastrophic) appraisals. Table 5 summarizes the various factors that maintain OCD symptoms.

Misinterpretations of one's thoughts might include any appraisal of the intrusive thought as personally significant or threatening. An example is the belief that thinking about bad behavior is morally equivalent to performing the corresponding behavior (e.g., "Thinking about committing adultery is as bad as actually doing it"). An international group of researchers interested in the cognitive basis of OCD, the Obsessive Compulsive Cognitions Working Group (OCCWG; Frost & Steketee, 2002) identified three domains of "core beliefs" thought to underlie the development of obsessions from normal intrusive thoughts. These are summarized in Table 6. Figure 1 graphically depicts the contemporary cognitive-behavioral conceptual model.

Table 6
Domains of Pathogenic Beliefs in OCD

Belief	Description
Inflated responsibility/ Overestimation of threat	– Belief that one has the power to cause and/or the duty to prevent negative outcomes featured in intrusive thoughts. – Belief that negative events associated with intrusive thoughts are likely and would be insufferable.
Exaggeration of the importance of thoughts and need to control thoughts	– Belief that the mere presence of a thought indicates that the thought is significant – Belief that complete control over one's thoughts is both necessary and possible.
Perfectionism/ Intolerance for uncertainty	– Belief that mistakes and imperfection are intolerable. – Belief that it is necessary and possible to be 100% certain that negative outcomes will not occur.

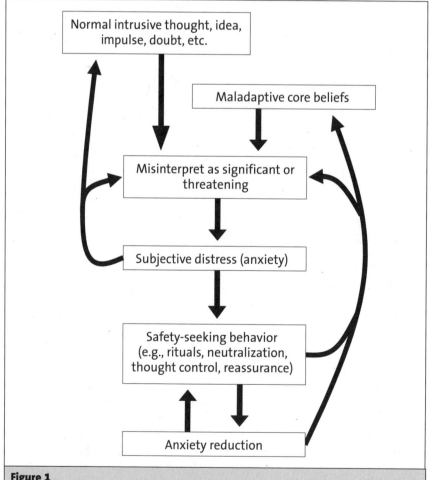

Figure 1
Cognitive-behavioral conceptual model of OCD

Implications of the Cognitive-Behavioral Model
Normalizing Effects
The cognitive-behavioral approach provides a logically and empirically consistent account of OCD symptoms that assumes the presence of intact learning (conditioning) processes and normally functioning (albeit maladaptive) cognitive processes. There is no appeal to "chemical imbalances" or disease states to explain OCD symptoms. Even the maladaptive beliefs and assumptions that lead to obsessions are viewed as "mistakes" rather than "disease processes." Furthermore, avoidance and safety-seeking rituals to reduce perceived threat would be considered adaptive if harm was indeed likely. However, OCD patients' obsessive fears are exaggerated. Therefore, their avoidance and safety-seeking rituals are not only irrational, but highly problematic since they perpetuate a vicious cycle of intrusion → misappraisal → anxiety, and so on.

The cognitive-behavioral approach assumes no specific brain dysfunction

Vulnerability to OCD
The distal cause of OCD is unknown, but the disorder's etiology probably involves interactions among biological, genetic, and environmental variables. Cognitive-behavioral models propose that certain experiences lead people to develop core beliefs that underlie OCD. For example, an obsession could develop in someone who was taught high moral standards and expected to obey rigid and extreme codes of conduct where the threat of punishment for disobedience was constantly present (e.g., certain religious doctrines). However, empirical evidence supporting the role of these kinds of experiences in the etiology of OCD is equivocal.

Treatment Implications of the Model
The cognitive-behavioral model leads to specific targets for reducing OCD symptoms. In particular, effective treatment must help patients (a) correct maladaptive beliefs and appraisals that lead to obsessional fear and (b) decrease avoidance and safety-seeking behaviors (e.g., rituals) that prevent the self-correction of maladaptive beliefs. In short, the task of cognitive-behavior therapy (CBT) is to foster an evaluation of obsessional stimuli as nonthreatening and therefore not demanding of further action. Patients must come to understand their problem not in terms of the risk of feared consequences, but in terms of how they are thinking and behaving in response to stimuli that objectively pose a low risk of harm. Those with aggressive obsessions must view their problem as lending too much significance to meaningless intrusive thoughts (instead of how they are going to achieve the ultimate guarantee that feared consequences will not occur). Patients with washing rituals must see their problem not as needing a sure-fire way to prevent illness, but as the need to change how they evaluate and respond to situations that realistically pose a low risk of illness. The treatment procedures outlined in Chapter 4 are derived from the learning and cognitive-behavioral models of OCD, and therefore address these targets.

Treatment implications of the cognitive-behavioral model

3

Diagnosis and Treatment Indications

This chapter provides the clinician with a framework for conducting a diagnostic assessment and providing consultation regarding treatment for OCD. The cognitive-behavioral model and its treatment implications (see Chapter 2) determine how information about the patient's symptoms is assessed and conceptualized. The initial consultation provides an excellent opportunity to initiate rapport building and begin socializing the patient to the cognitive-behavioral approach to OCD.

3.1 Form Versus Function

The cognitive-behavioral model emphasizes functional aspects of OCD symptoms

Whereas the diagnostic criteria for OCD emphasize the **form** of obsessions and compulsions (e.g., repetition), the cognitive-behavioral model emphasizes the **functional aspects** of these phenomena. From this perspective, the essential features of OCD are **anxiety-evoking** obsessional thoughts and **anxiety-reducing** strategies such as rituals and avoidance. It is the person's dysfunctional beliefs and appraisals of obsessional stimuli which give rise to obsessional fear. Thus, ways in which patients give meaning to obsessional stimuli must be assessed. Rituals and avoidance are deliberate attempts to reduce the anxiety evoked by obsessions. Yet whereas "compulsiveness" and repetition might be the most outwardly observable signs of OCD, patients actually deploy a variety of escape and

Safety behaviors in OCD

Table 7
Types of Safety Behaviors Observed in OCD

Type	Examples
Passive avoidance	Avoidance of situations and stimuli (e.g., driving, being the last one to leave the house, toilets, "666")
Compulsive rituals	Hand washing, checking, seeking assurances, repeating routine activities
Covert neutralizing	Mental rituals (e.g., repeating prayers, "good" words, or "safe" phrases), brief mental acts (e.g., canceling out a "bad" thought with a "good" thought)
Brief or subtle "mini" rituals	Use of wipes or paper towels, quick checks of appliances, scrutinizing others' behavior or facial expressions

Table 8
Common OCD Symptom Presentations

Symptom presentation	Commonly observed symptoms
Contamination	Obsessions concerning contamination from dirt, germs, body secretions, household items, poisonous materials; washing and cleaning rituals, avoidance
Harming	Obsessions concerning responsibility for injury or harm to others; compulsive checking, seeking assurance, repeating activities to prevent disasters
Incompleteness	Obsessions concerning order, asymmetry, imbalance (perhaps the fear that discomfort will persist indefinitely); compulsive arranging, ordering, repeating
Unacceptable thoughts	Obsessional thoughts, impulses, images of sex, sacrilege, and violence; mental rituals, neutralizing, seeking assurance

avoidance behaviors in response to obsessional distress, and only some of these tactics (collectively termed "safety behaviors") are repetitive or "compulsive". Table 7 shows the array of safety behaviors that might be observed in OCD. Clinicians should assess how the patient's safety behaviors are related to obsessional stimuli and dysfunctional thinking patterns.

Evidence for the functional relationship between obsessions and safety-seeking behaviors comes from research consistently identifying **dimensions** of OCD symptoms that involve specific types of obsessions and safety behaviors (McKay et al., 2004). Table 8 shows the most commonly identified OCD symptom dimensions.

3.2   The Diagnostic Assessment

The cognitive-behaviorally focused diagnostic interview begins with the patient providing a general description of his or her problem as well as the reasons for seeking help. Be sure to ascertain the functional relationship between obsessions and rituals as described in previous sections. Also, determine the onset, historical course of the problem, social, developmental, and medical history, and personal/family history of psychiatric treatment, along with substance use (i.e., drugs, alcohol, tobacco), and exercise and sleep habits. In addition, assess the treatment history (particularly treatment for OCD) as this may influence your current recommendations. Once this information has been obtained, use the Y-BOCS, BABS, HRSD, and various self-report measures to gather additional severity data.

Two additional self-report instruments, the **Obsessional Beliefs Questionnaire (OBQ)** and the **Interpretations of Intrusions Inventory (III)** (Obsessive Compulsive Cognitions Working Group, 2003), can be administered to assess OCD-related dysfunctional beliefs (i.e., those described in Table 6). The OBQ and III are reprinted in Frost and Steketee's (2002) edited volume on cognitive aspects of OCD.

When patients report
only obsessions or
only compulsions

Clinical Pearl
When Patients Report Obsessions or Compulsions in Isolation

Whereas the majority of OCD patients readily describe obsessional fears and compulsive rituals, some present with complaints of "pure obsessions" or "compulsions without obsessions." When assessing such patients, keep in mind that both obsessions and compulsions are present in the vast majority of people with OCD. Thus, you might need to conduct a more in-depth functional analysis. For individuals reporting only obsessions, this means inquiring about the use of any anxiety-reduction strategy (mental rituals or subtle behavioral or cognitive neutralizing or avoidance) that might be functioning to maintain obsessional fear. Most patients don't recognize these safety behaviors as OCD symptoms, but these behaviors maintain obsessional fear just as surely as overt rituals. If these phenomena are not present, perhaps the "obsessions" are not intrusive or anxiety-evoking and therefore not indicative of OCD (e.g., perhaps they are depressive ruminations, worries as in GAD, or other ego-syntonic thoughts).

When patients describe compulsive behaviors but fail to define obsessional fear, inquire about what triggers these behaviors. If they are not evoked by specific intrusive or distressing thoughts or situations as described in Chapter 1, OCD might not be the correct diagnosis. Perhaps an impulse-control (e.g., trichotillomania) or tic disorder is present. You should use the Y-BOCS checklist, self-report questionnaires, and detailed inquiry regarding the functional aspects of reported symptoms to rule in or rule out the diagnosis of OCD.

3.3   Identifying the Appropriate Treatment

3.3.1   Empirically Supported Treatments for OCD

Currently, two empirically supported treatments exist for OCD: cognitive-behavioral therapy (CBT) and pharmacotherapy involving serotonin reuptake inhibitor (SRI) medication. This section briefly describes these treatments and their advantages and disadvantages.

Medication for OCD
Table 9 displays the brand names, generic names, and therapeutic doses of medications with demonstrated clinical efficacy for OCD. These agents are thought to reduce OCD by increasing the concentration of serotonin. On average, a 20%–40% improvement in OCD symptoms over a 12-week period can be expected from treatment with medication. There are various advantages and disadvantages to using medication for treating OCD, and these are listed below:

Advantages of Medication
• Safe and easy to use
• Clinically effective: 20% to 40% symptom reduction on average

Disadvantages of medication
• Limited improvement rates
• About 50% of people do not improve
• Possibility of side effects
• Must be used continuously in order to sustain any improvement

Table 9
Medications with Demonstrated Clinical Efficacy for Treating OCD*

Brand name	Generic name	Therapeutic dose
Anafranil	Clomipramine	Up to 250 mg/day
Zoloft	Sertraline	Up to 200 mg/day
Prozac	Fluoxetine	40–80 mg/day
Luvox	Fluvoxamine	Up to 300 mg/day
Paxil	Paroxetine	40–60 mg/day
Celexa	Citalopram	Up to 60 mg/day

* At least one double-blind randomized controlled trial exists in which the medication was more effective than a placebo.

Cognitive-Behavior Therapy for OCD

CBT is based on an understanding of the **symptoms** of OCD (rather than its putative **causes**). Consistent with the cognitive-behavioral model (Chapter 2), OCD is viewed as a set of maladaptive thinking and behaving patterns that patients must learn to weaken. The vital components of CBT include (a) education, (b) cognitive therapy techniques, (c) exposure therapy, and (d) response prevention. These components are briefly described next.

The psychoeducational component of CBT for OCD entails socializing the patient to the cognitive-behavioral conceptual model and providing a rationale for how the treatment techniques are designed to weaken obsessions and compulsions. Cognitive techniques for OCD involve rational discussion to help the patient identify and correct mistaken beliefs that underlie obsessional fears, avoidance, and safety-seeking behaviors.

Exposure and response prevention are the centerpiece of the treatment program. **Exposure** entails gradually confronting situations and thoughts that evoke obsessive fear. This is often accompanied by imagining the feared consequences of exposure. For example, an individual who fears contamination and sickness from garbage cans would practice touching garbage cans and then imagine coming down with an illness from "germs." The procedure requires that the patient remain exposed until the associated distress decreases on its own, without attempting to reduce the distress by withdrawing from the situation or by performing compulsive rituals. Thus the **response prevention** component of CBT entails refraining from any behaviors (behavioral and mental rituals, subtle avoidance, and neutralizing strategies) that serve to reduce obsessional anxiety or terminate exposure. For example, the patient described above would refrain from any cleaning rituals. Exposure and response prevention provide the patient with evidence that obsessional fears are irrational and that rituals are not necessary to prevent disasters or reduce distress.

As with medication treatment, there are advantages and disadvantages to CBT. These are listed as follows:

Advantages of CBT

- Clinically effective: 60%–70% symptom reduction on average
- Treatment is fairly brief (usually 15 to 20 sessions)
- Long-term maintenance of treatment gains

Disadvantages of CBT
- Patient must work hard to achieve improvement
- Involves purposely evoking anxiety during exposure
- Not widely available

3.4   Factors that Influence Treatment Decisions

Factors that influence decisions about treatment

This section considers factors that influence clinical decisions regarding which type of treatment to recommend for a particular patient with OCD.

3.4.1   Age

CBT is the treatment of choice for all age groups with OCD. Compared to young and middle-aged adults, children and the elderly tend to have more difficulty with adherence to medication. The elderly are more vulnerable to drug side effects due to reduced metabolic rate and possible interactions with other medicines. Family conflict can interfere with CBT in children.

3.4.2   Gender

Men and women respond equally well to CBT. However, some patients feel more comfortable with a therapist of the same sex, especially if sexual or contamination concerns are present (e.g., fears of touching one's genitals). A same sex therapist would also be necessary to accompany patients during exposure to public restrooms.

3.4.3   Race

Some members of minority groups are uncomfortable receiving psychological treatments and prefer pharmacotherapy over CBT, as the former carries less stigma. Such individuals might be less willing to report embarrassing symptoms to the therapist or perform exposure tasks in public settings. Despite these issues, many minority patients with OCD achieve clinically significant improvement with CBT (Williams, Chambless, & Steketee, 1998).

3.4.4   Educational Level

Successful CBT requires that the patient grasp a theoretical model of OCD and a rationale for treatment. Patients must also be able to implement treatment procedures on their own and consolidate information learned during exposure exercises. These tasks may be difficult for individuals who are very concrete in their thinking. Medication is recommended for developmentally disabled and cognitively impaired patients.

3.4.5   Patient Preference

Patient preference
should be considered

Preference for a particular treatment modality should be considered. Reviewing the advantages and disadvantages of each approach allows the patent to make an informed decision about which therapy they would prefer to receive. Greater adherence to either treatment (especially CBT) can be expected from patients who agree willingly to a particular plan, as opposed to those situations in which treatment is forced on them.

3.4.6   Social Support

Although it may be beneficial for patients to identify a relative or close friend to provide support during CBT, this is not always essential. Such a confidant should be firm, relaxed, and empathic. Emotionally overinvolved, hostile, and inconsistent people can lead to treatment attrition. Before enlisting a specific support person to help with CBT, one should assess how this person interacts with the patient.

3.4.7   Clinical Presentation

CBT targets obsessions and compulsions. Thus, if such symptoms are not primary complaints, CBT is not recommended. Because CBT requires a substantial commitment, it should not be initiated when patients are concurrently engaged in therapies likely to compete for time and energy. Instead, such patients should begin with SRIs until their schedule can accommodate CBT.

In general, OCD symptom severity should not factor into the decision of whether to treat patients with medication or CBT. CBT is more effective than medication for any severity level. However, severe symptoms may require a more intense regimen of whatever treatment is offered: i.e., a higher dose of medicine or more frequent CBT sessions. If the patient presents a danger to self or others, inpatient treatment is recommended. Where possible, however, we recommend CBT be conducted on an outpatient basis to maximize generalizability of treatment gains to the patient's own personal surroundings.

3.4.8   OCD Symptom Theme

Both CBT and medication can produce improvement across the various presentations of OCD (e.g., washing, checking). However, these treatments appear less beneficial when hoarding symptoms predominate the clinical picture (Abramowitz, Franklin, Schwartz, & Furr, 2003). It also has been suggested that OCD patients with "pure obsessions" (i.e., obsessions without overt rituals) fare less well in CBT compared to those displaying overt compulsive rituals. However, as is described in Chapter 4, exposure and response prevention can be adapted to successfully treat this presentation of OCD.

Most presentations
of OCD respond to
CBT and medication

3.4.9   Insight

Patients with poor insight into the senselessness of their OCD symptoms show an attenuated response to CBT due to (a) reluctance to engage in treatment exercises and (b) difficulty consolidating what is to be learned from repeated exposures. While CBT is worth attempting, increased use of cognitive therapy techniques might be necessary to help patients engage in (and benefit from) exposure tasks. Another augmentative approach is to use medication; some psychiatrists use antipsychotic medication to treat patients with very poor insight.

3.4.10   Comorbidity

OCD patients with comorbid depression and those with GAD show reduced response to CBT. Seriously depressed patients become demoralized and have trouble complying with treatment instructions. Their strong negative affect may also exacerbate OCD symptoms. In GAD, pervasive worry detracts from patients' mental resources available for learning skills in CBT.

Other Axis I conditions likely to interfere with CBT are those that involve alterations in perception, cognition, and judgment, such as psychotic and manic symptoms. Patients actively abusing psychoactive substances are also poor CBT candidates. These problems impede the ability to profit from CBT exercises and can also reduce adherence. Bringing these comorbid conditions under control is a requirement before beginning CBT.

Both CBT and medication may be adversely affected by severe Axis II psychopathology. Different personality disorder (PD) clusters may differentially influence the process and outcome of CBT. Anxious (e.g., OCPD) and dramatic (e.g., histrionic) traits interfere with rapport development; yet, success is possible if a therapeutic relationship can be established. Patients with personality traits in the odd cluster (e.g., schizotypy) present a challenge to CBT due to their reduced ability to consolidate corrective information from exposure or cognitive interventions.

3.4.11   Treatment History

Patients who have received an adequate dosage of one SRI for a reasonable time (at least several weeks) are generally unlikely to respond to other SRIs, or to combinations of SRIs. Thus, for medicated patients who have not had psychological treatment, CBT is the logical recommendation. If patients report that they have undergone CBT, the adequacy of this therapy course should be assessed before making additional recommendations. If treatment sessions were infrequent, or if therapist-guided exposure and response prevention were not incorporated, a course of adequate CBT should be considered. On the other hand, a history of adherence problems may suggest the need for residential treatment or a supportive/interpersonal approach.

3.5   Presenting the Recommendation for CBT

Once you have determined that a patient is a candidate for CBT, present him or her with a summary of the assessment results and a rationale for starting treatment. At the patient's discretion, members of the patient's family (e.g., spouse or parent) who can be counted on to provide support can be included in this discussion. The points below should be clearly conveyed to the patient during this consultation.

How to recommend CBT to the patient

- Review the data collected during the interview which suggest the presence (and severity level) of OCD.
- Define OCD and review the signs and symptoms as discussed in Section 1.1. Use the patient's own symptoms as examples. Emphasize that OCD is a chronic problem that is unlikely to get better without effective treatment.
- Tell the patient that the exact causes of OCD are unknown. Some research suggests there is a biological basis (i.e., serotonin irregularities); other research suggests anxiety problems can be learned. Emphasize that numerous factors (biological and environmental) probably contribute to the development of OCD.
- Convey that effective treatment does not require that we know the causes, but only that we understand the **symptoms** of OCD. Fortunately, after much research, we have come to understand these symptoms very well.
- Describe medications for OCD, including their advantages and disadvantages, using the material presented in Section 3.3.1. Explain that medication is based on the biological model of OCD as a problem with serotonin.
- Describe CBT as a form of treatment that aims to weaken the **symptoms** of OCD, regardless of what causes them in the first place. Specifically, CBT aims to weaken two maladaptive patterns: (a) becoming anxious over obsessional triggers, and (b) using avoidance and compulsive rituals to reduce anxiety. Give examples of the patient's symptoms to illustrate these patterns.
- Using the information in Section 3.3.1 as a guide, describe the procedures of gradual exposure and response prevention. Inform the patient that these techniques involve learning skills to weaken the two patterns mentioned above. Provide examples of the kinds of exposure exercises and response prevention rules that might be used in treatment.
- Explain that during treatment, the patient can expect to become anxious, but that the anxiety is temporary and it subsides with practice. During treatment, the therapist will help the patient learn healthier ways of thinking and responding to anxiety-evoking situations so that the OCD patterns are weakened.
- Assure the patient that you realize CBT is hard work. Review the advantages and disadvantages to this approach.
- Use the analogy of the therapist as a **coach**. You will help the patient to learn and use skills to reduce OCD. This is accomplished in a collaborative manner. You will never force (or surprise) the patient with exposure tasks.
- Ensure that the patient understands that how much benefit a person gets from CBT is related to how much effort they put into doing the treatment.
- Recommend a trial of 16 sessions of CBT and answer any questions from the patient (and family members).

4

Treatment

4.1 Methods of Treatment

This chapter presents the nuts and bolts of how to plan and implement a CBT program for OCD. Table 10 shows the optimal schedule for what is to be accomplished in each treatment session. In our clinic, such a program is deliv-

Table 10
Suggested Session Structure in Psychological Treatment for OCD

Session 1
- Begin functional assessment of OCD symptoms
- Introduce self-monitoring
- Begin psychoeducation

Session 2
- Continue functional assessment
- Psychoeducation
- Cognitive therapy
- Begin planning for exposure

Session 3
- Psychoeducation
- Cognitive therapy
- Finalize and agree on the exposure treatment plan

Sessions 4–8
- Exposure (progressing up the fear hierarchy)
- Response prevention
- Cognitive therapy

Sessions 9–11
- Exposure (facing the greatest fears)
- Response prevention
- Cognitive therapy

Sessions 12–14
- Exposure (emphasis on patient as his/her own therapist)
- Response prevention
- Cognitive therapy

Sessions 15 & 16
- Final exposures
- End response prevention
- Assess outcome
- Arrange for follow-up care (as necessary)

ered in 16 twice-weekly sessions over an 8-week period (patients traveling from out of town receive 5 daily sessions for 3 consecutive weeks). However, in the interest of flexibility, the focus of this chapter is on mastery of the particular treatment **strategies** rather than on promoting a strict session-by-session agenda.

4.1.1 Functional Assessment

Functional assessment is the collection of highly detailed patient-specific information about obsessional triggers and the cognitive and behavioral responses to these stimuli, including a complete description of all compulsive rituals (behavioral and mental). The cognitive-behavioral theory dictates what information is collected and how it is organized to form a conceptualization of the problem and an effective CBT program. The **Functional Assessment of OCD Symptoms** form (see Appendix) is used to document this information. Depending on the complexity of the patient's symptoms, this assessment might last from 1 to 4 hours. Begin by providing a rationale for the detailed functional assessment that incorporates the following points:

Functional assessment—the collecting of detailed, patient-specific information

- CBT involves learning skills to weaken OCD symptoms.
- To tailor the program to the patient's specific obsessions and rituals, you must have a complete understanding of these symptoms.
- Treatment therefore begins by generating a list of all of the situations and thoughts that evoke anxiety and urges to do rituals.

Assessing Obsessional Stimuli
Generate a complete list of external triggers and internal stimuli (thoughts) that evoke obsessional fear. These stimuli might be used as the basis of exposure exercises.

External Triggers
Identify all objects, situations, places, etc. that evoke obsessional fear and urges to ritualize. Examples include bathrooms, knives, doing paperwork, churches, the number "13," leaving the house, driving in certain places, and so on. Examples of questions to elicit this information include:
- What kinds of situations make you feel anxious?
- What kinds of things do you avoid?
- What triggers you to want to do rituals?

Obsessional Thoughts
In OCD, anxiety is also evoked by recurring ideas, images, doubts, and impulses that the patient finds upsetting, immoral, repulsive, or otherwise unacceptable. Examples include thoughts of germs and contamination, impulses to desecrate the church, images of genitalia, ideas concerning loved ones being injured, doubts about making mistakes, and impulses to harm innocent people or loved ones. Examples of questions to elicit this information include:
- What intrusive thoughts do you have that trigger anxiety?
- What thoughts do you try to avoid, resist, or dismiss?

Assessing Cognitive Features

Obtain information about the following parameters of the cognitive basis of the patient's fear. This helps in developing effective exposure and cognitive therapy interventions.

Feared Consequences

Identify fears of disastrous consequences

Most patients articulate fears that something terrible will happen if they are exposed to their obsessional stimuli or if they fail to perform certain rituals. For example, they would be responsible for injury to a loved one, become ill (if they do not wash), have bad luck from confronting the number "13," or make terrible mistakes in paperwork. Examples of questions to elicit feared consequences include:

- What is the worst thing you imagine happening if you are exposed to (obsessional trigger)?
- What do you think might happen if you didn't do your _____ rituals?

Misinterpretations of Obsessional Thoughts

Identify the ways in which the patient misinterprets obsessional thoughts

Identify mistaken beliefs about the presence and meaning of intrusive obsessional thoughts, impulses, and images. For example, "Thinking about stabbing my wife could lead me to actually stab her," "God will punish me for thinking immoral thoughts," "I'm a pervert if I have unwanted thoughts about sex," and "Anyone who thinks gay thoughts must be gay." Examples of questions to elicit this information include:

- What do you think it means that you have this thought?
- What will happen if you think this thought too much?
- Why do you try to avoid or dismiss these thoughts?

Fears of Experiencing Long-Term Anxiety

Some patients do not articulate specific feared consequences, but instead worry that anxiety will persist

Some patients fear that anxiety (and anxiety-related bodily sensations) will persist indefinitely or spiral "out of control" if rituals are not completed. For example, "If I don't re-arrange the closet, I will never get over the feeling that things aren't just right." Questions to help elicit these types of cognitions include:

- Do you worry that you will become anxious and that the anxiety will never go away?
- What might happen to you if you remained anxious for long periods of time?

Because this type of fear is not always readily apparent to the patient, some patients have difficulty articulating that what they fear is actually the experience of feeling very anxious (i.e., sensations associated with the fight/flight response). These individuals might require prompting to be able to describe such concerns (e.g., "Some people with OCD have the fear that if they don't ritualize, their anxiety will go on endlessly and spiral out of control. Do you worry about this?").

Assessing Responses to Obsessional Distress

Determine the patient's maladaptive response to obsessional fear

It is essential for the therapist to determine the patient's maladaptive responses to obsessional fear (i.e., neutralizing, safety-seeking rituals) because such behaviors maintain OCD. All safety-seeking behavior (even covert responses) must be targeted in response prevention.

Passive Avoidance

Most patients avoid situations and objects associated with obsessions in order to prevent feared disasters. Examples include avoidance of certain people (e.g., cancer patients), places (e.g., public washrooms), situations (e.g., using pesticides, bathing one's infant), and certain words (e.g., "murder"). Pay particular attention to subtle avoidance habits such as staying away from the **most used** surface or refraining from listening to music while driving. Ascertain the cognitive basis for avoidance (e.g., "if I listen to music, I might not realize it if I hit a pedestrian"). Examples of questions to elicit this information include:

- What situations do you avoid because of obsessional fear?
- Can you ever confront this situation?
- How does avoiding _____ make you feel more comfortable?

Overt Compulsive Rituals

List all ritualistic behaviors including cleaning, checking, repeating actions, arranging objects, and asking for reassurance. Attend to inconspicuous behaviors such as wiping, the use of special soaps, and visually checking. Determine the cognitive basis for rituals (i.e., the relationship between rituals and feared consequences). For example, checking to prevent fires and using a certain soap to target certain kinds of germs. Examples of questions to elicit this information include:

- What do you do when you can't avoid (insert situation)?
- Tell me about the strategies or rituals you use to reduce obsessional fear of (insert obsessional fear).
- How does doing this ritual reduce your discomfort?
- What might happen if you didn't engage in this ritual?

Mental Rituals and Covert Neutralizing Strategies

Inquire about the use of mental rituals to neutralize unacceptable obsessional thoughts. Examples include thinking special "safe" thoughts, phrases, and images; repeating prayers in a set (or "perfect") way; mentally reviewing (over

Inquire about mental rituals and other covert neutralizing strategies

---

Clinical Pearl
The Play-by-Play Description

To gain additional insight into the patient's experience and how he or she copes with symptoms, you can ask for a "play-by-play" description of a few specific instances of obsessional fear, avoidance, and ritualistic behavior. This technique could also be used to focus the assessment on a particular symptom you are having difficulty understanding. It involves asking questions such as, "What was the context in which obsessional distress was evoked?" and "What was the first sign of trouble?" Patients are asked to step through the situation and report their emotional and cognitive responses. What were they feeling and thinking? What happened next? How anxious did the patient become and what did they do to reduce this anxiety (rituals, avoidance)? How did the situation resolve itself and how did they feel afterwards? You can also point out the relationships between obsessions and increased distress, and between rituals or avoidance and anxiety reduction. Illustrating to the patient how these symptoms are related (as opposed to being bizarre or "out of control") can instill hope in the therapy program, as well as a sense of trust in your expertise.

Ask the patient for a "play-by-play" description of OCD symptoms to illustrate a typical episode

and over) one's actions to allay obsessional doubts; and habitual thought suppression and mental distraction. Ascertain the cognitive links between mental rituals and misinterpretations of particular obsessional thoughts. For example, repeating the phrase "God is good" to avoid punishment for having sacrilegious thoughts, and suppression of violent thoughts to prevent acting violently. Examples of questions to elicit this information include:

- What kinds of mental strategies do you use to dismiss unwanted thoughts?
- What might happen if you didn't use the strategy?

4.1.2   Self-Monitoring

Self-monitoring is an important (and often overlooked) component of CBT

To aid the functional assessment, ask the patient to use the **Self-Monitoring Form** (see Appendix) to keep a real-time log of triggers that lead to rituals between sessions. Explain the form's importance and give instructions for completing it during the initial treatment session. Some patients fail to carefully and accurately self-monitor because they do not appreciate the task's relevance to treatment (many see it as "busy work"). To increase adherence, convey the following:

- Self-monitoring helps both the therapist and the patient gain an accurate picture of the time spent engaged in, and situations that lead to, rituals.
- It helps the patient identify obsessions and rituals that he or she might not be aware of.
- Some patients use the fact that they have to report their rituals to the therapist as motivation to resist the rituals.
- Accurate reporting of rituals between now and the end of treatment will reveal how much progress is made in therapy.

With the patient's input, choose which rituals will be monitored (i.e., the most prominent ones). Then, give the following instructions:

- Rather than guess, use a watch to determine the exact amount of time spent ritualizing.
- To avoid forgetting important details, record each ritual **immediately**, rather than waiting until the end of the day (or worse, right before the next session).
- Write a **brief** summary of the situation or thought that evoked the ritual.

A useful way to train patients to self-monitor is to review a recent ritualistic episode (or an "imaginary day") with the patient and have him or her practice recording the date and time, situation or thought that evoked the ritual, and the amount of time spent ritualizing. To further increase adherence, tell the patient that the first item on the agenda for the next session will be to review the self-monitoring forms.

4.1.3   Psychoeducation

The educational component of CBT helps the patient learn to conceptualize OCD symptoms based on the cognitive-behavioral model. It also teaches the patient how these symptoms are weakened by the techniques used in CBT (e.g., exposure). The main concepts to be conveyed are: (a) unwanted intrusive thoughts are normal, (b) dysfunctional interpretations of intrusive thoughts cause obsessions, (c) avoidance and compulsive rituals maintain obsessions, and (d) there is a coherent rationale for CBT. This rationale is especially important since patients who do not see how exposure and response prevention ultimately produce benefit can not be expected to fully engage in these challenging CBT techniques.

Begin by helping the patient to understand OCD symptoms as patterns that can be broken with practice. Convey the following points:

- The treatment techniques are based on the idea that OCD is a set of patterns of thinking and behaving that become a vicious cycle and that require help to break.
- Maladaptive thinking patterns in OCD involve overestimating the danger associated with obsessions, which leads to feeling anxious when certain situations and thoughts are encountered.
- The anxious feelings lead to urges to do something to reduce the anxiety or to prevent something bad from happening.
- The maladaptive behavioral patterns include rituals and other strategies that reduce obsessional anxiety.
- Rituals are counterproductive because they only reduce anxiety temporarily, yet in doing so, become stronger and stronger habits.
- The OCD thinking and behaving patterns can become so intense over time that they become disruptive in your life.

The next sections present modules for socializing patients to the cognitive-behavioral model of OCD and its treatment.

Normalizing Obsessional Thinking

Unwanted, senseless, or bizarre intrusive (obsessional) thoughts, ideas, or images are present to some degree in all presentations of OCD. Sometimes these thoughts are triggered by external stimuli (e.g., knives, toilets), whereas at other times they may be unprovoked (unwanted sexual images). Explain to the patient that such thoughts (no matter how repugnant or upsetting), are normal experiences for over 90% of the population. People with OCD habitually misinterpret these thoughts as highly significant, whereas nonpatients correctly disregard them as "mental noise." It may be helpful if therapists share examples of their own experiences with intrusive thoughts to demonstrate the normalcy of these experiences and to model acceptance of such "strange" occurrences. Most patients are surprised and relieved to find out that just about everyone has unwanted intrusive thoughts.

If the patient wants to know **why** people have strange or unwanted thoughts in the first place, explain that the human brain is highly developed and capable of enormous creativity. People can imagine all kinds of scenarios—some pleasant, and others unpleasant. For example, many people daydream of winning the lottery or scoring the winning touchdown in the Superbowl. Just as our "thought generator" produces positive thoughts that are unlikely to come true, it can also spawn unpleasant thoughts.

Underscore that the problem in OCD is not that obsessional thoughts occur per se, but how the person **appraises** these thoughts as very meaningful or

Psychoeducation helps socialize the patient to the cognitive-behavioral approach to OCD

Explaining the functional relationship between obsessions and rituals

Everyone has obsessional thoughts

threatening. Thus, the aim of treatment is not to eliminate obsessional thoughts altogether, but rather to correct the misappraisals and reduce the amount of **distress** associated with these normally occurring experiences. Once intrusive thoughts are no longer perceived as threatening, it won't matter when or how frequently they occur. Give the patient the **Everyone has Intrusive Thoughts** handout (see Appendix) to be read after the session is over. The handout reviews this didactic information and includes a list of intrusive thoughts reported by people without OCD.

Normalizing intrusive thoughts is useful for individuals with any OCD symptom subtype, although the most straightforward application is for unacceptable aggressive, blasphemous, and sexual obsessions, and with intrusive doubts. For patients with contamination symptoms this exercise can be used to normalize images of germs and doubts about illnesses. Senseless thoughts and ideas concerning the "need" for order, symmetry, balance, and exactness can also be normalized this way.

Patients may point out that although everyone has intrusive thoughts, their own intrusions are more frequent, more distressing, and more intense compared to those of nonsufferers. This is true, and it is therefore important for patients to understand how their own detrimental thinking patterns (which they can learn to change) are the real culprit. Dysfunctional beliefs cause normal intrusive thoughts to escalate into highly distressing and recurrent obsessions.

The Role of Dysfunctional Interpretations in OCD

Dysfunctional beliefs and interpretations give rise to emotional distress

The idea that emotional and behavioral responses are determined by one's **beliefs and perceptions** about situations (not by situations themselves) forms the philosophical basis of CBT. Patients must understand the process by which their dysfunctional beliefs and interpretations can lead to emotional responses, such as anxiety. Strong emotions, in turn, exacerbate obsessional thinking.

According to Beck's cognitive model, dysfunctional thinking may occur on two levels. **Automatic thoughts** are in-situation appraisals that go through a person's mind and provoke an emotional or behavioral response. For example, when someone with obsessions about germs drops a coin on the floor they may think, "I'll get sick if I touch the coin and don't wash my hands." **Dysfunctional assumptions**, on the other hand, are general underlying beliefs that people hold about themselves and the world which make them inclined to interpret specific situations and stimuli in a catastrophic manner. For example, the beliefs "I am highly susceptible to illness" and "if I think it, it will happen" would evoke distress and urges to ritualize if one had to pick up a coin from the floor. Unlike automatic thoughts, dysfunctional assumptions usually do not enter a person's consciousness during the anxiety-evoking situation.

Helping the patient understand the relationship between thoughts and emotions

The vignette that follows illustrates the use of Socratic dialog in which the therapist helps the patient understand how her thinking dictates her emotional and behavioral responses. After illustrating this model using a situation that is not emotionally charged, the next step is to apply it to an OCD-relevant situation. The patient in the example had an excessive fear that she would catch the herpes virus from a particular coworker who once had a cold sore on her lip.

Clinical Vignette

Illustration of the Cognitive Model with NonOCD-relevant Situation

Therapist: Suppose you and a friend plan to meet for dinner at 7:00 p.m. and it is now 7:30 p.m. and your friend hasn't shown up or even called to say that she'll be late. If you conclude that your friend decided that she doesn't like you anymore and therefore that you're a loser, how will you feel?

Patient: Sad or depressed.

Therapist: Right. How about if you believed your friend was being late on purpose just to jerk your chain?

Patient: Then I'd feel angry.

Therapist: Sure. How about if you thought that your friend had been in a terrible accident?

Patient: I'd be worried.

Therapist: Exactly. Do you see the importance of your thinking?

Patient: Yes. Depending on how I interpret the same situation, I could feel different emotions.

Therapist: That's right. The way you think about situations influences your emotional responses. So, *you*, not situations, have control over your emotions. This is called the "cognitive model of emotion."

Clinical Vignette

Illustration of the Cognitive Model with OCD-relevant Situation

Therapist: Now, let's see how the cognitive model might apply to OCD situations. You said that you become anxious and feel like washing your hands and changing your clothes whenever you are near this coworker. What kinds of thoughts would cause you to feel so anxious like you have to do these rituals?

Patient: I think that cold sores are easy to get from other people, so I assume I would probably get a cold sore if I came anywhere near her. On the other hand, if I wash and change, I won't get any cold sores.

Therapist: Do you see how your assumptions about the probability of you getting a cold sore lead to anxiety and the urge to do compulsive behaviors to prevent cold sores?

Patient: Yes, I see that.

Therapist: You said that other people don't wash themselves or change after interacting with this coworker. What must they be assuming about cold sores to keep them from feeling anxious or from having to do these rituals?

Patient: They probably don't think about it; or they just assume they won't get a cold sore unless there's intimate contact.

Therapist: Yes, that would make sense. Can you see that if you learned to think the same way, your coworker wouldn't seem so threatening anymore, and you wouldn't feel like you had to ritualize to stay safe?

Patient: I understand, but I can't just change my mind. I mean, I'm better safe than sorry, right!?

Therapist: That's what therapy is going to help you with. We're going to work together to help you interpret these kinds of situations in ways that will be more effective for you. For now, though, it is important that you see how the cognitive model works. Your thinking patterns are what cause your anxiety.

As we have seen, the anxiety evoking stimuli in OCD are often intrusive thoughts. Applying the cognitive model with thoughts as triggers can be tricky since these stimuli, and the maladaptive beliefs and interpretations, are all mental events. Therefore, you should help the patient to distinguish between (a) intrusive obsessional thoughts and (b) automatic thoughts or appraisals of these intrusions as in the following example. The patient was devoutly religious, yet experienced intrusive sacrilegious thoughts such as "Jesus wasn't perfect" and "the Church isn't perfect." He interpreted these thoughts as meaning that despite strong devotion to his faith, he was really a fraud who deserved to be excommunicated from the church.

Clinical Vignette

Distinguishing Between Intrusive Obsessional Thoughts and Automatic Thoughts

Therapist: You said that when these thoughts come to mind, you believe that you are really a fraud and that you need to stop yourself from thinking these thoughts. Can you see how you are *interpreting* your unwanted thoughts as very threatening?

Patient: Yes, I see that.

Therapist: How do you think those interpretations make you feel? What do they make you do?

Patient: They make me feel guilty, so I avoid churches and I am always praying for forgiveness.

Therapist: Right. So, the question is, Do these *unwanted* and *senseless* thoughts really mean you are a fraud? Do you really need to stop them in order to be a devout Catholic? Think back to what we discussed about those kinds of intrusive thoughts.

Patient: Well, if most people have unwanted thoughts, I guess *you* would say there's nothing wrong with having them. But that seems strange. I've worried about those thoughts for so long.

Therapist: That's because you have believed for a long time that those thoughts *are* very important. But actually, they aren't. In fact, they're not even consistent with how you really feel about your religion. Everyone now and then has ideas that conflict with their personal beliefs and morals. The real problem is not that you *have* these kinds of thoughts, but rather how you *misinterpret* them as very significant and threatening. In therapy, I will teach you about healthy ways to interpret these kinds of thoughts so that they become less frequent, less intense, and less distressing.

The Role of Avoidance and Safety-Seeking in Maintaining OCD

Explaining how safety-seeking behavior maintains obsessional fear

Patients must understand how their avoidance and safety-seeking behaviors (rituals, and other forms of neutralization) contribute to the vicious cycle of OCD. This will provide a rationale for response prevention. Discuss the following points with the patient.

- Review how obsessions increase anxiety and compulsive rituals temporarily decrease anxiety.
- Aside from compulsive rituals, there are other strategies that individuals often use that have the same effect as rituals. These include avoidance and subtle (mini) rituals (i.e., neutralizing).
- These strategies are collectively termed **safety-seeking behaviors** because they lead to feeling safe—like something awful has been avoided.

- Avoidance and rituals might seem strange, bizarre, or "out of control." Help the patient view them as anxiety-reduction strategies. Give an example of how rituals are used to neutralize obsessional anxiety. Make sure the functional relationship between obsessions and compulsions is understood.
- Rituals would be adaptive responses if there were real danger present. But, obsessional fear is based on **misinterpretations**. So, these responses are unnecessary and counterproductive.
- Avoidance tricks patients into thinking that they have averted catastrophe (give examples of the patient's avoidance patterns; e.g., "if you avoid touching the bathroom door with your hands, and you don't get sick, you will think that it's because you didn't touch the door"). Avoidance also keeps the patient from learning that the feared situation isn't really dangerous.
- When obsessional stimuli can not be avoided, the next best solution is to search for a way to **escape** from the feared situation and relieve the anxiety as quickly as possible in any way that seems to work (provide examples of how the patient's rituals are used to escape from obsessional fear). Because the escape strategies also reduce distress, they develop into patterns (negative reinforcement).
- Neutralizing strategies are another maladaptive response to obsessions that provide a temporary escape from distress, but that make things worse in the long run (give examples of the patient's neutralizing responses). Neutralizing also increases preoccupation with obsessional thoughts.
- In summary, safety-seeking behaviors are responses to obsessions that seem helpful in the moment, but that backfire in the long run.
- Treatment will weaken these patterns by creating opportunities for the patient to learn that safety behaviors are not necessary to reduce anxiety or prevent negative outcomes.

Clinical Pearl
Integrating Psychoeducation into the Functional Assessment

A useful way to think about the initial sessions of CBT is as an exchange of information between patient and therapist. On the one hand, the patient is an "expert" on his or her particular OCD symptoms and must help the therapist understand the nuances of these symptoms in order that an individual treatment plan can be developed. On the other hand, the therapist is an expert in conceptualizing OCD symptoms and must teach the patient to understand his or her symptoms in a way that best fosters benefit from the treatment procedures.

In our clinic, we explain this situation to patients at the very beginning of the functional assessment phase. We weave the psychoeducational component into this assessment by capitalizing on any opportunities to help the patient understand the functional aspects of his or her symptoms. For example, when assessing obsessional thoughts, if a patient describes his or her intrusive thoughts as "strange" or "abnormal", or insinuates that he or she is the only person with such thoughts, we begin educating him or her immediately about the normalcy of unwanted thoughts. This technique helps socialize the patient to the cognitive-behavioral model of OCD, which is critical for a positive treatment response.

Integrating psychoeducation into the functional assessment

Presenting the Rationale for CBT

Presenting the rationale for using the specific CBT techniques to reduce OCD

Once the patient has a grasp of the cognitive-behavioral model, present a rationale for CBT by discussing the following points:

- The treatment techniques, **exposure** and **response prevention**, are designed to weaken the maladaptive thinking and behavior patterns in OCD.
- Exposure involves gradually confronting situations and thoughts that evoke anxiety. Response prevention involves refraining from doing anything to get rid of obsessional anxiety, except staying exposed to the situation.
- Give examples of specific exposure and response preventions exercises that might be prescribed for the patient.
- The basic idea of exposure therapy is simple. Repeatedly confronting situations and thoughts that evoke anxiety helps the patient learn that anxiety does not remain at high levels or spiral "out of control." Instead, distress actually **subsides**. This is called **habituation**. Since the patient usually escapes from the feared situation (by doing rituals) before anxiety subsides, he or she never has the opportunity to see that habituation eventually occurs.
- Therapy also helps the patient learn that obsessional fears are unlikely to occur even if no rituals are performed.

How to explain the concept of *habituation*

Draw a graph similar to that in Figure 2 to depict the within- and between-sessions habituation curves over the course of several exposure sessions. Discuss the graph as follows:

- The patient should expect to feel anxious at times, especially when starting to confront the feared situation. But this distress is temporary—it will eventually subside if the patient remains in the feared situation without using safety behaviors.
- The graph shows what happens with repeated and prolonged exposure. At the start of the first session, discomfort increases and then declines as

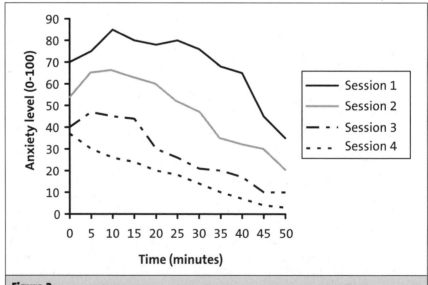

Figure 2
Expected pattern of within-session and between-sessions habituation during repeated exposure

time passes. At the second session, the discomfort subsides more quickly because learning has occurred. After several exposure trials the initial distress level is lower and it subsides even more quickly because the patient has learned that the situation is not highly dangerous. With repeated practice, the feared situations no longer provoke anxiety.

- This pattern only occurs if the exposure exercise is carefully designed and if the patient remains exposed for a long enough time without performing rituals (i.e., the patient must "invest anxiety now in order to have a calmer future").
- There are two kinds of exposure. **Situational** or **in vivo** exposure means facing the actual feared situations. **Imaginal exposure** means facing fears in imagination.
- Exposure with response prevention is often very helpful for OCD, but it is hard work and must be done correctly in order to get good results.

Next, discuss how you will work with the patient to tailor the treatment program to his or her needs.

The patient should understand that treatment is tailored to his or her specific OCD symptoms

- The patient will help the therapist make a list of exposure stimuli that will be put in order from less anxiety-provoking situations to those that are more difficult.
- Exposure exercises will be planned ahead of time as to avoid surprises.
- The therapist will provide support and coaching during each exposure task.
- Sometimes, treatment instructions might seem especially risky, or involve doing (or thinking about) things that most people wouldn't ordinarily do (or think about) on purpose. The patient must understand that the purpose of exposure and response prevention is not just to practice doing what **most people** do. These tasks are designed to weaken OCD symptoms.

The relationship between patient and therapist in CBT is analogous to that between a student and a teacher, or between a ballplayer and a coach. In the example below, the therapist explained his role as similar to that of a music teacher.

The therapist is essentially the patient's "coach" for overcoming OCD

Clinical Vignette
Describing the Patient/Therapist Relationship

Therapist: The best way to think of me is as your coach. Let's say you wanted to learn to play a musical instrument like the drums. You would go to a drum teacher who would give you instructions and then watch you play to look for things that you need to work on. The teacher would then help you improve your technique and tell you to practice hard between lessons. Now, if you didn't practice the new techniques, or if you practiced them in a different way from how the teacher taught you, you would not develop the skills needed to be a good drummer. Also, the teacher would not force you to practice—you would decide whether or not to practice. If you didn't practice, the teacher might encourage you to practice more, but eventually he or she might stop the lessons if it was clear that you weren't practicing enough.

> Treatment for OCD goes the same way. I know how to create exercises that are designed especially for you to reduce your obsessions and rituals. If you practice these exercises the way that I show you, chances are you will see improvement. But, if you decide not to practice them as much as you should, or if you decide to change the exercises around, chances are you will not improve as much as you would like. I have a great deal of confidence in this treatment. But, I can not force you to do the exercises—this is your therapy and the decision has to come from you. What I *will* do is help you see that your feared situations are not as dangerous as you think, and that it is in your best interest to approach, rather avoid them. We are on the same team against OCD. If you do the hard work in therapy, you will find that my coaching and support is very helpful.

4.1.4   Using Cognitive Therapy Techniques

Using cognitive therapy techniques

Cognitive therapy techniques for OCD teach patients to identify, evaluate, and modify dysfunctional thinking patterns (i.e., maladaptive beliefs and assumptions) that give rise to obsessional fear and compulsive urges. Patients are helped to develop realistic beliefs about anxiety-evoking situations and thoughts.

What is the role of cognitive therapy in CBT for OCD? Research shows that cognitive techniques by themselves have limited efficacy in reducing OCD symptoms. However, cognitive therapy can play a role in helping to facilitate assessment, preventing premature discontinuation, and maximizing adherence with exposure therapy (Kozak & Coles, 2005). I suggest using cognitive therapy strategies to "set the table" for exposure and response prevention. That is, to "tenderize" dysfunctional beliefs and assumptions to the point that the patient can more readily engage in and profit from exposure exercises. Ways of integrating cognitive therapy with exposure are discussed below.

Discussing and Challenging Cognitive Distortions

Identifying ways in which the patient misinterprets situations and thoughts raises awareness of how such thinking patterns lead to obsessional fear. Instead of providing didactic information or reassurance, you should promote **collaborative empiricism** by asking relevant questions to help the patient discover for him or herself an understanding of how maladaptive thinking patterns maintain OCD symptoms. The Appendix provides a list of **cognitive distortions** present in OCD. Review this handout in the session and explore with the patient how these thinking styles might play a role in his or her particular symptoms. The text below presents modules for challenging some of these maladaptive thinking patterns.

Intolerance of uncertainty

Avoidance and safety-seeking behavior in OCD represent attempts to guarantee safety. It is as if patients believe the absence of complete reassurance of safety implies a high risk of harm (in contrast, nonsufferers assume situations are safe if clear-cut danger signs are absent). Put another way, people without OCD have the adaptive ability to **feel** certain about many things despite the fact that absolute certainty is more or less an illusion. You can use the following demonstration to illustrate this problem:

Clinical Vignette

Clarifying the Function of Avoidance and Safety-Seeking Behavior in OCD

Therapist: Think about your mother [who is not in the room]. Is she alive right now?

Patient: Of course. Why do you ask?

Therapist: I'm interested in how you know she's alive *for sure*?

Patient: When I was in the waiting room I talked with her on my cell phone.

Therapist: But that was 20 minutes ago. Isn't it possible that something terrible could have happened since then?

Patient: I guess so... So, maybe I don't know for *certain* that she's alive. But, I would *bet* that she's OK.

Help the patient understand how intolerance of uncertainty contributes to OCD

Point out that it is impossible to be 100% certain in this (and in most situations). Medical emergencies, etc., **can** occur. Yet, in this experiment, the patient based his judgment on a **probability** as opposed to a **guarantee** of safety. Next, discuss other low probability "risks" that the patent takes on a regular basis (e.g., driving home from the session) to demonstrate that the patient knows how to properly manage uncertainty. To reduce OCD symptoms, however, he or she must be willing to practice living with uncertainty about obsessional fears as well.

Intolerance of uncertainty underlies obsessional fears of events that might occur in the **distant future** (e.g., cancer from long-term exposure to pesticides, going to Hell). Patients often argue that they "cannot take the chance" of the feared event coming true. Here, you can point out that they would benefit by developing an alternative, less threatening, interpretation of the experience of uncertainty. This is illustrated in the example below of a patient with obsessional fears of becoming schizophrenic:

Clinical Vignette

Managing Fears of Future Events

Therapist: How have you been reacting to your doubts about becoming schizophrenic?

Patient: Like I can't take the chance that I might go crazy.

Therapist: Right; and where does that lead you?

Patient: I get worried so I ask everyone for reassurance.

Therapist: Right. If you apply the same strategy that you say you used when I asked you about your mother, what could you tell yourself about those doubts that would help reduce OCD?

Patient: That the thoughts *probably* do not mean I am becoming schizophrenic.

Therapist: That's right, they're *probably* just "mental noise". You would be better off accepting *some* uncertainty since a 100% guarantee that you'll never develop schizophrenia is not possible.

Overestimation of threat

People with OCD tend to exaggerate the risk of harm associated with obsessional situations in two ways: by overestimating the (1) **probability** and (2) **severity** of the feared outcome. These thinking patterns fuel anxiety since they imply that danger is lurking. Cognitive techniques can help the patient develop more realistic ways of thinking about the potential for harm. An example of a Socratic dialog between a patient and her therapist is presented below:

Clinical Vignette

Example of a Socratic Dialog Looking at Overestimation of Threat

Therapist: So, you are afraid to use the toilet where you work?

Patient: Yes. It seems like there are lots of germs in the staff bathroom because many people use that toilet. It's not safe.

Therapist: What do you think would happen if you used the toilet?

Patient: I would catch a disease from the toilet seat.

Therapist: What kind of disease; and what would happen if you caught it?

Patient: I never thought about that exactly. I guess I would get so sick that I wouldn't be able to work.

Therapist: How about the other people at work. How do they feel about that particular toilet? Do they avoid it too?

Patient: No. I've seen most of them go into that bathroom.

Therapist: So, I guess these other people must get sick a lot, right?

Patient: [thinks]... Well, not really. Everyone is pretty healthy.

Therapist: Hmm. So, what do you think it means if other people who use that bathroom stay healthy?

Patient: Maybe it's not as dangerous as I think. I never thought about it *that* way before. But still, what if I am more susceptible to germs than other people? Doesn't it make sense to avoid it just to be on the safe side?

Therapist: Well, I agree with you that the toilet is probably not as dangerous as you think. What is it that makes you think you are more susceptible to germs than someone else might be?

Patient: Nothing really. I guess I'm just afraid of the germs.

Therapist: I'm glad you recognize that you have been overestimating the dangerousness of the toilet. Do you see the cognitive distortion here? That is what leads you to be afraid. When we do exposure practice you will learn that you are probably no more or less at risk than other people who use that bathroom.

Sometimes patients reason that although feared outcomes may be unlikely, they **could** occur; so taking precautions such as avoidance and rituals is prudent ("better safe than sorry"). Such thinking indicates that the patient is still ignoring pertinent evidence to the contrary. Patients may also believe that avoidance and safety-seeking rituals have prevented feared outcomes. For example, a patient with unwanted impulses to harm her baby might say that she did not act on the violent thought **because** she neutralized it with a "safe" thought. Such arguments call for revisiting the psychoeducational module explaining the mechanisms by which compulsive behavior maintains overestimates of threat.

Overestimation of responsibility

Some patients have an inflated sense of their power to cause or prevent negative outcomes (e.g., "if I don't pray that my loved ones are safe, it is as bad as pur-

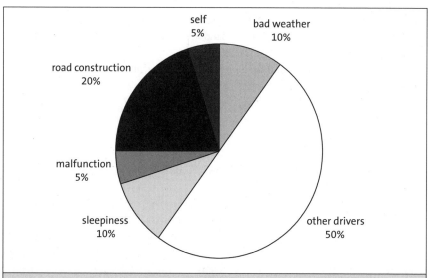

Figure 3
Illustration of the pie chart method for a patient with obsessions concerning responsibility for accidents

posely injuring them"). You can help such individuals gain perspective on their degree of responsibility for feared outcomes by having them identify all possible contributing factors and then rating how much each factor contributes (what percent) to the overall responsibility for such an event. This information can be incorporated in a pie chart to visually illustrate the logical error as in Figure 3.

The patient in this example had obsessional fears that she would be responsible for her boyfriend dying in a car accident. She felt she had to ritualistically "bless" him by saying certain prayers in order to prevent such a catastrophe. The therapist asked the patient to list factors, other than herself, that might contribute to an accident. The patient cited bad weather, other drivers, sleepiness, a car malfunction, and road construction. Next, the percent responsibility attributable to each of these contributions was rated and drawn in as pieces of the pie. The leftover part of the pie was labeled as the patient's own contribution (5%) and she was able to see that by her own rating, her responsibility for the feared outcome was minimal.

Significance of thoughts (thought-action fusion)
Beliefs that merely **thinking** blasphemous, aggressive, or sexual thoughts is equivalent to "immoral" behavior indicate the need for additional discussion regarding the normalcy (and unimportance) of intrusive upsetting thoughts. Ask the patient what she or he thinks of the fact that even virtuous, ethical, and kind people sometimes have similar "bad" thoughts. If a double standard is present, this should be pointed out and alternative explanations can be discussed.

If the patient believes that unwanted thoughts will **lead** to the corresponding event, explore his or her ideas regarding the mechanism by which this could occur (e.g., "How do you think your thoughts of stabbing your baby will lead you to commit this action?" "How will thinking about your sister having a car accident make it happen?"). Inconsistencies with reasoning can then be explored through Socratic questioning to encourage the patient to re-think such assumptions (e.g., "If thoughts lead to actions, how are people able to maintain control of themselves when they get angry?" "Can you recall a time when you thought of something and it didn't happen?").

If the patient is concerned that such obsessions imply he or she is a dangerous or immoral person, the discussion can focus on the "kinds" of people who would and would not be upset by violent, blasphemous, or sexual thoughts. Unlike the patient, someone intent on committing violence would not worry if they had thoughts about such behavior. A pervert would not be upset by sexual impulses. An atheist would not be concerned over sacrilegious images. Does the patient have a history of behavior or thoughts consistent with these obsessions? (probably not).

You can use the following experiment to further illustrate this point: Hand the patient a delicate object and ask him or her to **think about** throwing the object across the room. When he or she does not throw the object, discuss the various factors that contribute to performing actions (e.g., decision-making). Thoughts, by themselves, do not translate to impulsively engaging in behaviors. This and other similar exercises (e.g., going outside and "wishing" for car accidents, buying a lottery ticket and thinking of winning) demonstrate that one need not worry about intrusive senseless thoughts.

Need to control thoughts

The need to control thoughts follows from dysfunctional beliefs about the importance of thoughts

The need to control thoughts follows from beliefs about the overimportance of thoughts. However, if patients are unaware of how their attempts at thought control are destined to fail, they might believe that their mind is "out of control." One technique for demonstrating the futility of attempts to control unwanted thoughts is to engage the patient in the following experiment:

How to demonstrate the futility of trying to suppress obsessional thoughts

Therapist: Let's try an experiment. I'd like you to try *not* to think of a pink elephant for one minute. You can think of anything else in the world *except* for a pink elephant. OK? Go.

Invariably, the patient will have pink elephant thoughts and agree that it is nearly impossible to fully suppress them. Next, ask the patient to explain how this phenomenon applies to obsessional thoughts. Such a discussion should focus on how attempts to suppress obsessional thoughts lead to more unwanted distressing thoughts and even more futile attempts to suppress. Of course, suppression attempts are unnecessary since obsessional thoughts are not dangerous in the first place.

Perfectionism and the "just right" error

In discussing beliefs about perfection, help the patient recognize that such an "all-or-nothing" approach is futile since perfection is largely an illusion. Help him or her to identify instances (unrelated to OCD) in which perfection is not demanded and in which there is no associated distress. This means the patient knows how to manage imperfection, yet must learn to apply this where OCD is concerned.

Severe perfectionism can interfere with the completion of therapy assignments (e.g., "If I can't do it perfectly, there's no sense in doing it at all"). In such cases, instruct the patient to purposely complete such tasks **imperfectly** to test out whether feared outcomes (e.g., failure to benefit) really occur.

Clinical Pearl
Capitalizing on Opportunities to Maximize Cognitive Change

The liberal use of cognitive techniques throughout a course of CBT for OCD is encouraged. A few examples of how these strategies can be applied at various points appear below.

- During exposure exercises (described in Section 4.1.6), help the patient process his or her experience. Review evidence regarding the probability and severity of feared consequences that is gleaned by performing the exercise. Help the patient articulate more realistic beliefs about obsessional stimuli.

- When a patient shows strong affect, ask him or her to identify thoughts and images leading to their emotional response *at that moment*. Using Socratic questioning, address dysfunctional beliefs and assumptions. Apply this to OCD as well as to unrelated issues that may arise (e.g., a romantic break-up)

- Point out and summarize changes in beliefs during and after the completion of exposure exercises. Once the patient is socialized to the cognitive-behavioral model, ask him or her to provide such summaries.

- If self-monitoring forms indicate continued ritualizing, help the patient identify underlying dysfunctional cognitions. For example, "What were you saying to yourself when you saw the fire engine and decided to go home to check whether the appliances were unplugged?" and "What were the short- and long-term consequences of your ritualizing?"

Capitalizing on opportunities to maximize cognitive change

4.1.5   Planning for Exposure and Response Prevention

The aim of exposure and response prevention for OCD is to allow the patient to have experiences in which obsessional stimuli are confronted without the use of safety-seeking rituals, but where feared outcomes do not materialize and the only explanation is that the obsessional stimuli are not as dangerous as was thought. The **fear hierarchy** is a list of the situations, stimuli, and thoughts that the patient confronts during exposure sessions. Hierarchy items must match the patient's particular obsessional fears and they are ranked according to the level of distress that the patient expects to encounter during exposure to that particular item.

Building the Fear Hierarchy: Situational Exposure

Informed by the functional assessment, and with the patient's assistance, compose a list of between 10 and 20 situations that evoke the patient's obsessional fear. Record these situations in the top portion of the **Fear Hierarchy Form** (see Appendix). Suggestions for choosing suitable hierarchy items appear below. Examples of fear hierarchies appear in Chapter 5.

Designing the fear hierarchy

The guiding principle when deciding on exposure hierarchy items is that these situations and stimuli must closely match the patient's particular obsessional fears. Therefore, patients with contamination fears must confront items such as floors, elevator call buttons, toilet seats, shoes, door handles, feces, pesticides, hospitals, feared people (e.g., shaking hands), sweat, etc. Items that serve as reminders of contaminants (e.g., a book that belonged to a gay person) might also be incorporated if such stimuli are avoided. Exposure for patients with fears of mistakes or harm (negligence) might involve leaving the stove on and going outside, locking the door in a "careless" way, completing assignments hastily without checking for accuracy, driving on crowded streets, placing sharp objects on the floors in public places (fear of responsibility for accidents), or thinking curse words before writing important letters (fear of unknowingly insulting others). Individuals with fears of bad luck might confront "unlucky" numbers (e.g., 13, 666) or words (e.g., "death"), blasphemous phrases, or the Satanic Bible. Those with violent obsessions would confront items that trigger violent thoughts, such as knives. Those with sexual or religious obsessions would confront whatever stimuli evoke unacceptable ideas, such as pornographic material, religious icons, and the like. Finally, for patients with concerns about symmetry and order, exposure would entail confronting the kinds of imperfection, disorder, imbalance, etc. that the person tries to avoid. Details for how to conduct exposure to these various stimuli are provided in Section 4.1.6

Choose exposure tasks that represent "ordinary levels of risk" within the confines of your (or an expert's) judgment. Situations or stimuli that evoke the patient's worst obsessional fears must be included on the hierarchy. Failure to confront the worst fears reinforces the mistaken idea that such situations should be avoided because they really **are** too dangerous.

It is not essential that every possible fear cue appear on the hierarchy. Items should be detailed enough to advise the patient and therapist of the nature and difficulty of the exposure exercises, yet leave open the option to modify the specific task(s) in accord with the patient's specific fears. This permits flexibility in developing exposures of varying degrees of difficulty as needed (some of which might not be contrived until the particular exposure is begun). The vignette below illustrates how to include the patient in selecting items.

The best exposures are those which allow patients to test (and disconfirm) their fears of disastrous consequences (e.g., "I will hit people with the car").

Clinical Vignette

Putting Together a Fear Hierarchy

Therapist: You said that you limit your driving because you are afraid of hitting pedestrians. So, it sounds like a good situation for you to practice for exposure would be driving through the mall parking lot on a weekend afternoon.

Patient: Oh God, I couldn't do that! I'd be too afraid. Maybe I could do it on a weekday when there are less people around.

Therapist: Well, as you know, the point of exposure is to practice taking risks where you feel afraid. You will see that your anxiety subsides and that your fears are less likely to occur than you think. So, suppose we *begin* with driving through the parking lot on a weekday with the aim of progressing up to trying this exercise on a weekend? Avoiding the weekend scenario altogether would not be a good choice.

Patient: I know, but it's hard for me to do.

Therapist: That's why we will start with the easier of the two. I bet you'll feel better about trying it on the weekend once you try it and see that it's not as bad as you think.

However, in some instances feared consequences pertain to disasters in the distant future and are therefore not subject to immediate disconfirmation (e.g., going to hell when one dies). In such cases, exposure tasks should be designed with the understanding that the aim is to learn to tolerate acceptable levels of risk and uncertainty.

Once an initial list of items is generated, ask the patient to assign a numerical rating of subjective units of distress ("SUDS") for each item (i.e., "How anxious would you feel if you confronted _____?"). The SUDS scale includes every number from 0 (no distress) to 100 (maximal distress), although it can be introduced using the anchors shown below:

The SUDS scale

- 0 SUDS = no distress (like you are asleep).
- 25 SUDS = minimal distress.
- 50 SUDS = moderate distress.
- 75 SUDS = high distress.
- 100 SUDS = maximum distress (e.g., being tied to the railroad tracks as the train is coming around the bend).

Record the patient's SUDs rating for each item on the hierarchy form. Next, working with the patient, establish the order in which hierarchy items will be confronted (and record this on the hierarchy form). Some considerations for designing this treatment plan are as follows:

- Begin with moderately distressing items (e.g., 40 SUDS) and work gradually up to the most disturbing items.
- The most distressing items should be confronted during the middle third of treatment (about the 10th session).
- During the last third of treatment, exposure to the most distressing stimuli is repeated in different contexts. The patient also takes more of an active role in designing and implementing these later exposures.
- Items that were inadvertently omitted from the hierarchy can always be added after discussion with the patient.
- Each item is first confronted under the therapist's supervision and then practiced between sessions.
- Items may be omitted when they evoke little or no discomfort on two successive exposure trials.

Building the Imaginal Exposure Hierarchy

Imaginal exposure provides a systematic way of repeating and prolonging confrontation with intrusive obsessional thoughts, images, and urges that evoke anxiety. Scenes to be imagined are chosen from the list of obsessional thoughts and ideas of feared consequences generated during the functional assessment. Brief descriptions of these scenes, their SUDS ratings, and the order in which they will be confronted are entered onto the bottom part of the **Fear Hierarchy Form.**

There are three types of imaginal exposure. In **primary imaginal exposure**, the patient confronts anxiety-evoking intrusive thoughts, images, and urges which may or may not be evoked by external cues. Items typically include articulations of a distressing, graphic, vulgar, or sacrilegious obsessional thought, such as explicit stories of sexual or violent acts, or descriptions of accidents involving loved ones.

Imaginal exposure

Secondary imaginal exposure involves imagined confrontation with the feared consequences of not performing rituals. For example, imagining being responsible for the death of a loved one because rituals were not performed correctly. Secondary imaginal exposures usually correspond to a situational exposure item. For example, a patient with fears of fires might leave the iron plugged in (situational exposure) and, after leaving her home, purposely imagine that she has caused a serious fire.

Preliminary imaginal exposure involves visualizing confrontation with situations and stimuli before actually conducting situational exposure to that item. This sort of exposure is generally not planned during the hierarchy development phase, but instead is inserted as needed when conducting situational exposure. For example, if a patient is reluctant to engage in a situational exposure to sitting on the bathroom floor, you might suggest that he or she **imagine** doing this as a precursor to the actual exposure.

The Response Prevention Plan

The response prevention plan

Although the term "response prevention" engenders images of physically restraining patients from performing rituals, the procedure is fully voluntary. Optimally, the patient completely abstains from all rituals and neutralizing behaviors beginning with the first exposure session. However, some patients require a gradual approach to stopping. Key considerations when planning for response prevention appear below.

- Revisit the educational materials presented in earlier sections and emphasize the importance of **choosing not to ritualize**.
- Define the limits of response prevention and do not require that patients take more than acceptable risks. For example, if "no checking mirrors while driving" is a rule, allow for an exception when going in reverse (e.g., one brief check).
- Do not violate cultural or hygienic norms. Patients with washing rituals should be allowed to shower and brush their teeth each day. However, they should "re-expose" themselves to contaminants following a shower.
- Specify abstinence from "mini rituals" and subtle safety behaviors that might not initially be recognized (or reported) as OCD symptoms (e.g., reassurance-seeking).
- If relatives or friends are involved in the patient's rituals, encourage their help with response prevention.

Enlisting a designated support person for the patient

Clinical Pearl
Enlisting a Designated Support Person

Some patients encounter difficulty conducting exposure and response prevention tasks independently (between sessions). It may be useful in such cases to designate a "support person" such as a close friend or relative who agrees to be available for the patient to assist with treatment (when called upon by the patient). The support person should meet with the therapist to receive instruction in how to help with treatment. The best support persons are those who are able to be empathic yet firm. Individuals who are over-involved in the patient's symptoms, or who are overly critical or harsh, should be avoided. The support person is to report any adherence problems to the therapist.

- For patients who are initially unable to cease all rituals, consider a gradual approach in which instructions to stop rituals parallel progress up the exposure hierarchy (with the goal being complete abstinence midway through treatment).
- The patient must record violations of response prevention on Self-Monitoring Forms and report them to you. Violations indicate trouble spots that require additional work.

Some typical response prevention rules for common presentations of OCD are as follows:

Ideas for implementing response prevention for common compulsive rituals

Decontamination rituals

Patients are not to use water (i.e., no washing) or other cleaning agents (e.g., hand gels, wet wipes) on their body. Creams, make-up, bath powder, and deodorants are allowed as long as they are not used to reduce contamination fears. Water may be drunk or used when brushing teeth, but not to clean the face or hands (shaving should be done with an electric razor). One daily 10-minute shower is permitted, but ritualistic washing of specific body parts is not allowed (unless medical conditions necessitate such cleansing). Following the 10-minute shower, the patient must re-contaminate with items from earlier exposures.

Checking, counting, arranging, and repeating rituals

The patient is not to engage in any repetitive behavior. For example, only **one** brief glance in the rearview mirror when driving, **one** quick check of the door when leaving the home, **one** rapid proof for errors when completing paperwork, etc. Checking and counting are not allowed for items normally not checked (e.g., appliances) or counted (e.g., steps). Counting rituals may be foiled by counting incorrectly. Actions repeated because of the presence of "bad thoughts" (e.g., going through a doorway) must not be repeated. Arranging items that appear imperfect is not allowed.

Reassurance-seeking rituals

Compulsive reassurance-seeking from family members, "experts" (e.g., priests, doctors), or from the therapist, is not permitted. You will need to educate individuals from whom the patient habitually seeks reassurance about the need to refrain from answering questions during treatment. Suggest that they respond in a supportive way and refer the patient back to you. For example, "I'm sorry but I can't answer your question because I agreed to help you with treatment. What else could I do to help you manage your discomfort? Maybe you'd like to call your therapist about this?"

Mental Rituals

Patients are to refrain from mental strategies for canceling (neutralizing) or "putting right" unacceptable thoughts. Prayers, except as dictated by religious authorities, are prohibited. Permissible prayers are not to be repeated or used to deal with obsessional fear. Arranging response prevention for mental rituals requires a discussion with the patient. He or she might already have a method for blocking rituals. If mental rituals can not be easily stopped, you can suggest that the patient (a) think of an **upsetting** thought instead; or (b) perform the mental ritual in error. For example, if the ritual is to mentally reassure oneself by reviewing events (e.g., to be sure one did not say curse words in the synagogue), the review should be purposely foiled (e.g., "I *probably* said a curse word").

Agreeing on the Treatment Plan

The patient and therapist must agree on the treatment plan before CBT begins

The patient and therapist must both agree to adhere to the plans for exposure and response prevention. Review the following points before moving on:

- Beginning with the next session, the patient will practice facing the situations and thoughts listed on the exposure hierarchy.
- The patient will also practice refraining from rituals as planned. Resisting rituals will teach the patient more healthy ways to manage obsessional fear.
- Daily self-guided exposure tasks will be assigned for practice between sessions. These tasks may be practiced alone or with the supervision of a designated support person.
- The patient should expect to feel anxious when first facing each new situation, but must agree to follow the program without arguing with the therapist.
- The therapist will not force the patient into exposure tasks, but will encourage him or her to choose exposure instead of avoidance.
- The patient must prepare to "tough it out" when the going gets rough. Things may be challenging in the beginning, but they will get easier. The therapist will be like a coach that provides instruction and support throughout the program.
- The patient is expected to resist all urges to ritualize. He or she must contact the therapist (or the designated support person) before carrying out any rituals so that someone can help with resisting the urges.
- If an urge can't be resisted, the ritual should be recorded on the self-monitoring form. The patient must also immediately re-expose him or herself to the situation or thought which evoked the ritual.
- Treatment should not proceed until the patient agrees to this treatment plan.

4.1.6   Implementing Exposure and Response Prevention

Implementing exposure and response prevention

This section describes how to conduct exposure therapy for OCD. The basic format of each exposure session is outlined in Table 11. During exposure, the patient confronts the predetermined hierarchy item(s) and remains exposed, without performing any rituals or neutralizing behaviors, until the level of distress and urges to ritualize dissipate. The optimal duration of each exposure session is about 90 minutes.

Checking Homework and Reviewing Self-Monitoring Forms

Each exposure session should begin with a general check-in and review of homework assignments. All forms should be inspected and the patient should provide a qualitative report of his or her work between sessions. Following up

Table 11
Components of Exposure Sessions

Procedure	Approximate time
• Checking in • Checking homework • Reviewing self-monitoring forms	15 min.
• Conducting the exposure exercise	45–60 min.
• Agreeing on homework practice	5 min.
• Planning for the next session's exposure	10 min.

Components of
exposure sessions

Clinical Pearl
Goals for Early Exposure Sessions

To strengthen the patient's trust and participation in exposure therapy, you should appear knowledgeable, consistent, and confident. Showing an understanding of the patient's OCD symptoms, being up front when discussing the treatment procedures, and taking seriously the patient's input also helps strengthen the patient's conviction in the treatment program.

During initial exposure sessions, help the patient develop good "work habits" for performing these tasks by attending to (and shaping) the patient's behavior. Most will have never tried this type of exercise before. Explain why exposure is to be done in ways that evoke distress. Be democratic (as opposed to autocratic) and show sensitivity to help the patient view you as an advocate, rather than a taskmaster.

Goals for early
exposure sessions

on instructions for homework and self-monitoring reinforces the importance of working hard between sessions. It also helps you determine whether all instructions have been followed correctly. When the patient successfully completes (or demonstrates sufficient effort toward completing) assigned tasks, this should be rewarded with praise. Be sure to ask what the patent learned from completing the assignment. When assignments are not completed as instructed, troubleshoot and, if necessary, complete the homework in that day's session before moving on.

Reinforce the
importance of
homework by
checking the
patient's forms at the
start of each session

Introducing the Exposure Task
Begin by describing the specifics of the planned exposure task, including how the feared stimulus will be confronted, for how long, and what kinds of safety-seeking behaviors (rituals) are not permitted during and after the exercise. To give the patient an idea of how the exercise is to proceed, review **The 10 Commandments for Successful Exposure** handout (see Appendix) before proceeding with the first exposure. A brief description of the exercise and an initial SUDS rating should be entered on the **Exposure Practice Form** (see Appendix), which is used to keep track of progress during each exercise.

A typical introduction to an exposure task is as follows:

How to introduce the
exposure task

Therapist: At the end of our last meeting, we agreed that the exposure task
for today will be for you to practice writing words you've been avoid-

ing, such as "disease," "AIDS," and "cancer." We'll begin with easier words, but by the end of the session I'd like you to be writing even the most distressing words like "tumor" and "death." So, you will practice writing these words over and over on this pad of paper. I also want you to allow yourself to think about any disturbing images that may come to mind. You are not to "cancel out" these unwanted images, or use other strategies to make you feel less distressed. Just let the thoughts "hang out" in your mind. I know this is going to produce anxiety for you, but doing this exposure will help teach you that these words and thoughts are not dangerous; they will not lead to becoming ill. Also, you will see that your distress subsides if you don't try to fight the thoughts. It will also help you to gain a sense of mastery over your fear—and that would be a nice accomplishment. I will be keeping track of your anxiety level during the exposure by asking you to rate your SUDS level every five minutes. So, have in mind a number between 1 and 100 to give me. Are you ready?

From a cognitive angle, exposure corrects dysfunctional beliefs and interpretations of obsessional stimuli. Therefore, it is helpful to identify the patient's feared consequences of doing the exposure without ritualizing (e.g., "I will get cancer and die"). If negative consequences are not readily articulated, it might be that the patient fears that their anxiety or discomfort will persist indefinitely. The feared consequence, as well as the patient's estimates of probability and severity, is recorded on the **Exposure Practice Form** (see Appendix).

Prolonged and repeated exposure also results in habituation of anxiety within and between sessions. The **Exposure Practice Form** includes space for keeping track of the patient's SUDS levels at regular intervals through each exposure trial.

Conducting Exposure Exercises

How to conduct exposure exercises for common OCD symptoms

This section presents detailed instructions for conducting exposure tasks for common presentations of OCD.

Contamination Fears

Contamination exposures should begin gradually and progress according to how the patient is responding. Start by encouraging the patient to touch the feared contaminant. If necessary, during early exposures, you might model this by touching the stimulus yourself. The patient must **fully** confront the feared stimulus—briefly touching it with fingertips does not "count." The patient must feel thoroughly contaminated. He or she must also focus on, rather than distract from, the stimulus. Regularly asking questions such as "How are you feeling now?" "What are you telling yourself?" and "What's your SUDS?" helps maintain this focus.

The vignette on the next page illustrates exposure to a "contaminated" towel from the patient's home bathroom.

Amplifying refers to deliberately intensifying an exposure in order to address a particular aspect of avoidance. For contamination exposures, this usually means contaminating items or body parts the patient tries to avoid

Clinical Vignette

Example of an Exposure Exercise with Contamination Fears

Therapist: I'd like you to start by touching the towel. Use your whole hand.
Patient: [hesitates] ...OK. [holds on to the towel.] There.
Therapist: Good for you. So, how does it feel?
Patient: It's soft and dry. Dryer than I thought it would feel.
Therapist: How about *you*? How do *you* feel?
Patient: I'm a little nervous since this is the towel that was near the toilet when it overflowed.
Therapist: You're doing great. It's OK to feel anxious. That's the whole idea. It's worth feeling anxious now so that you will not be as afraid in the future. What is your SUDS rating?
Patient: About 50 [therapist records this on the form].
Therapist: How strong is your urge to wash your hands?
Patient: Pretty strong. Like 75%.
Therapist: You're doing very nicely. Keep holding on to the towel.

tainting (e.g., purse, wallet, face, hair, mouth). As an example, the patient above was instructed to put the towel in her lap and to touch it to her arms, legs, and face. This was repeated every 5 to 10 minutes until it evoked less discomfort. New areas were added at each amplification. For example, the patient touched the towel to her purse (inside and out), hair, and jacket.

Look for subtle avoidance and safety behaviors such as wiping, opening doors with one's feet, and other curious maneuvers that most people don't do. Patients who appear to "space out" during exposure should be asked whether they are engaging in distraction or other strategies such as praying and analyzing. These safety behaviors might be so habitual that they occur without the patient's awareness. Therefore, they must be brought to the patient's attention whenever they are observed.

The importance of matching the exposure situation to the patient's obsessional fear can not be overstated. Patients fearful of "spreading" contamination to other people can practice shaking hands with "innocent" others. Those fearful of "floor germs" can conduct entire sessions seated on the floor (in a public bathroom, if necessary). For those concerned with bodily waste and fluids, we supervise direct confrontation with such substances (or situations in which the substances **might** be present). Examples include, putting a drop of urine on the back of the hand and handling dirty towels from the gym locker room (fear of sweat).

Obsessional Doubts of Harm and Negligence

Carrying out exposure for harming symptoms is more complicated than for contamination symptoms. This is because harming obsessions and checking rituals are usually triggered by circumstances in which the patient perceives a risk of being responsible for causing or (failing to prevent) harm, injury, or damage. So, exposure in the presence of a therapist is not necessarily a bona fide exposure since the patient can transfer responsibility for any negative consequences onto the therapist.

To further complicate matters, many situational exposures for harming symptoms would be compromised if they are prolonged or repeated during the

Exposure for harming, injury, and mistake obsessions can be complex

same session. For example, plugging in the iron or turning on the stove can only be done once during a single session because repeating these exercises is inherently a check that no fire has started. Therefore, necessary precautions must be taken to ensure that no de facto reassurance seeking occurs that would invalidate the exposure. Instead of repeating such activities, a good solution is to have the patient perform them once, and then promptly leave the premises (without checking). The exposure can be prolonged using secondary imaginal exposure to images of the feared consequences.

Some examples of exposure assignments for patients with harming symptoms and checking rituals are as follows: A patient who fears hitting pedestrians can perform driving exposures without checking the roadside or mirror. Someone fearful of causing a fire or a burglary can practice turning off lights and appliances, or closing and locking doors, without checking. A patient with fears of stabbing others can use knives and pins around others. Someone with fears of cursing or insulting others can practice writing and saying curse words.

When the feared act of commission or omission presents a very low risk of harm, exposure can involve deliberately carrying out such behaviors. A few examples are as follows: a patient who fears that failing to warn others of glass on the floor will result in someone being injured can purposely place pieces of glass on the floor of a crowded area (and refrain from warning people). Someone fearful of starting a fire can intentionally leave appliances (even the stove) on and unattended for an acceptable period of time. A patient who fears miswriting an address on an envelope can purposely misspell the addressee's name, street, or city. A person who fears performing imperfectly could purposefully commit minor "imperfections" as exposure tasks. Someone afraid of numbers such as 13 or 666 can deliberately write these numbers on their hand or on pictures of people they would not want to "curse."

Secondary imaginal exposure should be integrated with situational exposure when patients report feared consequences of not ritualizing. For example, a patient with obsessional fears of leaving confidential information out on his desk at work first completed a situational exposure involving handling confidential files, putting them away, and leaving the room without double checking. Next, as a secondary imaginal exposure, he confronted obsessional thoughts of mistakenly leaving the files in the wrong place and being fired because others had viewed them. The imaginal exposure was introduced as follows:

Clinical Vignette
Introducing an Imaginal Exposure

Therapist: You said that when obsessional doubts of violating confidentiality come to mind, you often return to work to make sure you haven't left any confidential materials out on your desk. To help you learn healthier ways of responding to these obsessional doubts and urges to check, we are going to have you practice thinking the obsessional doubts, but instead of checking, you will allow the doubt and uncertainty to remain. You need to concentrate on the distressing thoughts and not try to remember for sure if you put the confidential materials away. By doing this exercise, you will see that your distress level eventually subsides even if you don't go back and check or try to mentally review

> your activities to reassure yourself. The goal is for you to learn that these obsessional doubts are simply "mental noise."
>
> We will do this imaginal exposure using a loop tape on which we will record your obsessional thoughts about the feared consequences of violating confidentiality. You will then listen to the tape until you no longer have significant anxiety or urges to check. Every now and then I will ask for your SUDS rating. .

The patient then wrote a description of his feared consequences of leaving confidential materials on his desk and failing to double check. The description was edited with the therapist to ensure that it contained elements that the patient experienced as most distressing, such as his irresponsibility for the breach of confidentiality, and the idea that he **should** have checked more carefully. The script was then recorded onto a 2-minute audio loop tape. The patient listened to the tape and visualized the scenes until his subjective distress declined.

Unacceptable Obsessional Thoughts

Exposure for unacceptable thoughts involves primary imaginal exposure to the obsessional thought, image, or impulse; and situational exposure to stimuli that provoke such obsessions. The patient remains exposed to the obsession, without neutralizing or performing rituals, until anxiety declines naturally (habituation). The example below illustrates how to conduct an exposure session for a patient with repugnant stabbing obsessions.

Using primary imaginal exposure for repugnant obsessional thoughts

Clinical Vignette

Introducing an Exposure Exercise for Unacceptable Obsessional Thoughts

Therapist: The exercise you will do for today's exposure will help you to weaken your pattern of becoming highly anxious when you have meaningless intrusive thoughts about stabbing people. We will start by having you describe the obsessional thoughts on a loop tape, which you will listen to until your distress subsides. You will also practice holding sharp objects, like a knife. Remember that you must not make any attempt to suppress, remove, or neutralize the unwanted thoughts. Instead, you need to embrace the thoughts and practice interpreting them as a normal part of you. If you do feel yourself trying to remove the thought, you need to let me know so I can help you remain exposed. The goal of this exercise is not to make the thoughts go away, but to give you the opportunity to learn that these kinds of thoughts are not dangerous and that your anxiety will eventually subside. I will keep track of your SUDS during the exercise.

The patient was first asked to write a script of her obsessional thoughts. After editing with the therapist (to highlight the most distressing aspects of the thoughts), the final version, which the patient recorded onto the loop tape, was as follows:

Sharp objects can be dangerous. I could use them to stab people, which would badly hurt or kill them. When I use knives, I often think of stabbing innocent people and people that I especially care about, like my husband, Greg. If people are not expecting to be stabbed, I could do terrible damage with just a few thrusts of a knife in the right place, such as their neck, eyes, chest, stomach, or genitals. If a person is not ready, they would not be able to fight back until it was too late and they would die of their stab wounds that I inflicted.

I could stab Greg while he was sleeping. He would be unaware that I was doing it until the knife pierced his skin and entered his body. He might wake up in terror and try to fight off my stabbing, but he would lose so much blood that he wouldn't be able to fight me off. I could easily kill him by stabbing him in his sleep. There would be blood everywhere and he would be screaming from all of the pain. If I stabbed him in the right place, I'd damage his vital organs and he would die.

The patient listened to the loop tape for 15 minutes and her SUDS decreased from 85 to 65. At that point, the therapist gave the patient a large butcher knife and asked her to hold it while listening to the tape. After an initial increase in SUDS to 70, her anxiety declined to 40 after another 20 minutes. At that point, the therapist introduced the patient to a coworker (who had volunteered to help with treatment). The loop tape was turned off and patient was instructed to hold the knife while talking with this confederate. Then, the confederate sat at a computer terminal while the patient held the knife to the confederate's back and elicited stabbing thoughts. Finally, this exercise was continued with the therapist out of the room, but checking in every 5 minutes to obtain a SUDS rating. When the patient's SUDS had declined to 25 (after 75 total minutes), the exposure was ended.

Incompleteness Symptoms

Patients with incompleteness symptoms may or may not articulate fears of harm. When the sense of inexactness, imperfection, or asymmetry evoke

---

Integrating cognitive techniques into exposure therapy

Clinical Pearl
Integrating Cognitive Therapy with Exposure

Prolonged and repeated exposure exercises help the patient develop more realistic estimates of the probability and severity of feared consequences. In addition, the decline in distress that accompanies therapeutic exposure helps to modify dysfunctional beliefs that anxiety will persist indefinitely. Cognitive therapy techniques should be used at various points during exposure sessions to facilitate these cognitive changes.

- **When initiating an exposure task**, cognitive techniques can be used to identify mistaken cognitions (e.g., "thinking about harm is the same as causing harm") and feared consequences (e.g., "I will be responsible for a terrible accident") that can be tested during exposure.

- **During exposures**, cognitive techniques can be used to promote adaptive beliefs and responses to obsessional fear (e.g., "Even if something happens, it's not my fault").

- **After an exposure exercise**, Socratic discussion is used to help the patient review the outcome of the exercise, examine evidence for and against the catastrophic beliefs, and develop more realistic beliefs about obsessional stimuli.

obsessional fears of responsibility for disasters (e.g., "Dad will die if I do not put on my clothes the 'correct' way"), exposure to external cues should be conducted, accompanied by secondary imaginal exposure to the feared consequences (as would be done in the case of harming obsessions). Patients must of course be reminded to refrain from rituals such as ordering and arranging, checking and repeating, and reassurance-seeking. One patient who worried that stepping on sidewalk cracks would cause harm to his parents purposely stepped on cracks and confronted thoughts of his parents being injured because of this. Another feared bad luck from odd numbers and therefore practiced facing them wherever possible by purchasing items that cost $7.99, and choosing to be 9th in line. He also practiced wishing for bad luck to occur as a result of his confrontation with odd numbers.

When the patient is mostly concerned that anxiety/distress will persist unless items (e.g., books, clothing) are arranged or ordered properly, exposure aims to desensitize the patient to the sense of incompleteness. With prolonged and repeated exposure to the "imperfection," the patient learns that the distress associated with these feelings fades over time, thereby rendering ordering rituals unnecessary.

Prescribing Homework Practice

At the completion of each in-session exposure, assign self-controlled (homework) practices for each day between sessions. Homework includes exposure, refraining from safety-seeking rituals, and continual self-monitoring of violations of response prevention. Consider the following points when designing homework assignments:

- Assign repetitions or variations of the in-session situational and imaginal exposure exercises.
- Provide copies of the **Exposure Practice Form** to be completed during each homework assignment. Specify the details of each assignment on the form.
- Suggest that the patient review **The 10 Commandments of Exposure** handout before beginning each exercise.
- Reinforce the importance of homework by beginning each session with a check of the previously assigned work.

> Conclude each treatment session by reviewing progress and discussing plans for the next session's exposure exercise

Planning for the Next Session

At the end of each session the therapist should review the patient's progress up the exposure hierarchy and discuss the task scheduled for the next session. If items need to be brought from the patient's home, or if the session must take place out of the office, this should be arranged. Such planning demonstrates your commitment to the therapy and reassures the patient that there will be no surprises. In short, it engenders trust and allegiance to the therapist and the therapy.

> Helping patients confront the most distressing exposure stimuli

Conducting Exposure to the Most Distressing Stimuli

Exposure to the most feared hierarchy items should be conducted during the middle third of the treatment program. This ensures ample therapy time to sort out unforeseen obstacles that arise while progressing up the hierarchy, or that surface when attempting to confront the most difficult stimuli. Deciding on a clear timetable for when these exposures will take place also helps the patient

Clinical Pearl
Helping Patients Confront their Greatest Fears

For many patients, success with early exercises predicts success with high-level exposures. However, if the going gets tough, convey sensitivity and understanding that such tasks are highly distressing; yet also reiterate that this **temporary** distress is a necessary part of therapy. You can use the following tactics to help patients who are having difficulty attempting the most difficult exposures:

- Model the task prior to instructing the patient to engage.

- Use intermediate exposures that are of greater difficulty than those already conducted, but not as difficult as the planned task (the patient must agree that the intermediate step serves to facilitate eventual exposure with the more difficult item).

- Use cognitive therapy techniques to identify and modify dysfunctional beliefs that are evoking high anxiety.

- Review evidence collected during previous exposures.

- Discuss the importance of learning to take acceptable risks.

- Revisit the importance of learning to tolerate uncertainty

understand the importance of carrying out these tasks on schedule. Consider that procrastination on the patient's part might be a form of avoidance.

Planning the most difficult exposures for the middle third of the program also affords ample time for repeating these exercises in varied contexts. Fear reduction is most complete and durable when feared stimuli are confronted in a variety of circumstances, as opposed to only in the therapist's office. Thus, after the most distressing hierarchy items have been confronted under controlled conditions, the remaining sessions should involve repetition of these exposures in varied contexts.

Programmed and Lifestyle Exposure: Encouraging Independence

Programmed and lifestyle exposure

The previous examples primarily illustrate **programmed** exposure in which the patient implements planned exercises under your direction at specific times and in particular locations. Yet patients must also engage in **lifestyle** exposure, which means making choices to take advantage of day-to-day opportunities to practice confronting (rather than avoiding) obsessional stimuli and **choosing to be anxious**. Encourage the patent to be opportunistic and to view spontaneously arising obsessional triggers as occasions to practice treatment techniques and work on further reducing OCD symptoms.

You should routinely remind patients that every choice they make regarding whether to confront or avoid an obsessional cue carries weight. Each time they choose to confront such a situation without using rituals, OCD symptoms are weakened. Yet, whenever a decision is made to avoid a potential lifestyle exposure situation, OCD symptoms are strengthened.

As it becomes clear that the patient has learned to correctly implement exposure independently, step back and encourage the patient to become his or her "own therapist." This means allowing the patient to design his or her own exposure tasks (e.g., by choosing from equally fear-evoking stimuli). Of course, the therapist has the last word regarding the nature of each exercise, and you must therefore monitor the planning and implementation of these tasks. This will also prepare the patient for life after therapy.

Stylistic Considerations
Remarks During Exposure Tasks

Offering appropriate observations, praise, encouragement, and support during exposure maintains the sort of rapport that is necessary for a successful outcome. Ask the patient to tell you what he or she is learning by doing exposures. When exercises are proceeding as planned (i.e., SUDS levels and urges to ritualize are decreasing), the following sorts of comments and open-ended questions are helpful:

What to say (and what *not* to say) during exposure sessions

- "You're doing great. Remember, if you remain exposed to a situation, your anxiety level decreases on its own."
- "It looks like you're much less anxious now compared to when we started the session; and you haven't done any rituals. How do you explain that your anxiety is lower?"
- "This seems like it's getting easier for you. You're weakening the link between obsessional thoughts and anxiety. Good for you."
- "You see, as I told you before, you don't need to engage in rituals to reduce your anxiety."

If the patient is having difficulty with anxiety during the exercise, convey understanding of how difficult exposure can be, and that with time and persistence, the exercises will ultimately become more manageable. Offer the following remarks:

- "Sometimes it takes a while for anxiety to go down. That means that you have to stick with the exposure even though it may be difficult. Eventually, you will begin to feel less distressed; You'll be glad you stuck with it."
- "This time your anxiety did not decrease by much, but we will keep working at it until it gets easier."

Avoid providing reassurance that exposure tasks are "not dangerous" or that the patient is "guaranteed" to be safe. These are things that the patient must learn for him- or herself. The example below illustrates a helpful and unhelpful way to address patient requests for reassurance during exposure.

Patient: Are you sure this is safe to do? Normal people wouldn't do a thing like this!

Unhelpful therapist response: Yes, it's OK. I promise. I wouldn't let anything bad happen to you. Just trust me.

Helpful therapist response: If you are asking me to guarantee you that the situation is absolutely safe, I can't do that. I don't know for certain what the outcome will be. But, I do know that all the evidence suggests that the risk is low enough that it's worth trying; especially if doing this exercise will help with your OCD…

Dealing with strong urges to ritualize

As individuals begin response prevention, they may have difficulty with strong urges to ritualize. Reviewing how such urges are learned responses to obsessional cues, and how they diminish over time even if resisted, is useful in helping the patient to resist violating response prevention instructions. The use of imagery, as in the example below, can also be helpful. This patient struggled with resisting compulsive urges to check door locks in her home.

Clinical Vignette

Using Imagery to Manage Compulsive Urges

Therapist: Is there something you could imagine—it doesn't matter what the image is—that will grab you and help you resist? Perhaps you could imagine spraying the urge with a fire extinguisher, or surfing on the urge until it crests and breaks.

Patient: [Smiling] I know what I can imagine—I could picture you standing in front of the door, waving your finger and shaking your head at me.

Therapist: That's great. Should I look mean?

Patient: No, just having you there will help me stop checking.

Therapist: That sounds like a good plan.

Humor

The use of humor or laughter to lighten the mood during exposures may be appropriate and can be beneficial, although it is not advised in times of extreme distress. Follow the patient's lead and ensure that remarks remain relevant to the exposure situation and do not distract the patient from the task.

Refining the Exposure Hierarchy

Sometimes, important details of the patient's obsessional fears do not become apparent until after the exposure hierarchy has been developed. Therefore, as treatment progresses, the therapist should remain alert for perviously unidentified situations and stimuli that trigger obsessions, avoidance, or that evoke compulsive rituals. Such situations should be incorporated into the exposure hierarchy.

Exposure "Field Trips"

The highly specific obsessions and avoidance behaviors of individuals with OCD often require that exposure exercises be conducted outside of the therapist's office. Such "field trips" might include visiting funeral homes, cemeteries, restaurants, places of worship, hospitals, stores, the patient's own home, etc. Ideally, the therapist has the flexibility to leave the office or meet the patient at the site where such exposures can take place. If not, perhaps a well-coached support person can accompany the patient of such trips. A final option is for the patient to check in with the therapist by cellular telephone while conducting the exposure tasks on his or her own.

Usually, exposures in public places can be conducted anonymously. The therapist and patient should plan in advance how the exercise will proceed so that directives can be kept to a minimum in public. Necessary behaviors such as touching or rearranging items should be performed discreetly so as not to draw undue attention. Unforeseen difficulties, such as high levels of anxiety or a persistent sales clerk, can be managed by leaving the scene, regrouping, and returning another time. In some situations it may be ideal to call ahead before visiting exposure situations. For example, calling ahead to let a funeral home manager know you will be dropping by. In this example, the patient explained that the purpose of this visit was to help her overcome her fears of funerals. When a cover story and plans for various contingencies (e.g., running into a friend) are discussed ahead of time, we find that most patients are willing to go out in public to conduct exposure with their therapist.

4.1.7 Ending Treatment

This section discusses a number of issues that should be addressed toward the end of therapy.

Concluding Response Prevention

As the last session nears, begin to discuss appropriate checking, cleaning, arranging, or praying behavior. As a rule, if such behaviors are performed in response to fears of negative consequences, they are probably rituals. Some examples of guidelines for resuming "normal" behavior after treatment appear below.

Helping the patient end response prevention and return to "normal" behavior

- Limit showering to one 10-minute shower per day. A second shower is permitted if there is extreme perspiration and body odor, or before getting dressed to go out (e.g., to a formal event). During any shower, wash each body part only once.
- Once the door is closed, you are allowed to turn the handle once to make sure it is firmly locked. Otherwise, no returning to check is allowed.

Assessing Treatment Outcome

In addition to informally assessing progress, evaluation of treatment outcome should include re-administration of symptom measures (e.g., Y-BOCS). Most patients will report some residual symptoms. Emphasize that "normal" obsessions and rituals are a part of everyday life for most people, so such experiences will never completely be absent. However, treatment has helped the patient learn to **respond** to obsessional stimuli in new healthy ways. Distress and functional impairment can be minimized with continued practice of the skills learned in treatment.

Obtain post-treatment ratings of symptom severity to accurately document progress in treatment

Continuing Care

Some patients desire additional treatment. As a general rule, those who have made little progress after 16 to 20 sessions of well-conducted CBT are unlikely to benefit further by adding additional sessions. Such individuals might be referred for supportive psychotherapy to help manage existing OCD symptoms. Attending a support group run by a local affiliate of the Obsessive Compulsive Foundation (www.ocfoundation.org), if available, is another good option. If residual OCD symptoms are minimal, yet there is concern about possible relapse, follow-up sessions can be considered (relapse prevention programs for OCD are described elsewhere (e.g., Hiss, Foa, & Kozak, 1994). Alternatively, a less formal strategy involving telephone calls and less frequent (perhaps monthly) appointments could be undertaken.

Preparing for Stressors

Patients should **expect** to experience residual OCD symptoms from time to time. Often, these are triggered by increased life stress, such as in the midst of occupational or family conflict, following a death or serious illness in the family, or around the time of childbirth. Help the patient identify potential "high risk" periods during which they should be ready to apply the techniques learned in therapy.

4.2   Mechanisms of Action

There are three mechanisms by which CBT may reduce OCD symptoms

From a behavioral perspective, CBT is thought to be effective because it provides an opportunity for the extinction of conditioned fear responses. Specifically, therapeutic (repeated and prolonged) exposure to feared stimuli produces **habituation**—the inevitable natural decrease in conditioned fear. Response prevention aids this process by blocking the performance of anxiety-reducing rituals, which would serve as a premature escape from anxiety. Extinction of conditioned anxiety occurs when the once-feared obsessional stimulus is repeatedly paired with the nonoccurrence of feared consequences and the eventual reduction of anxiety. From a cognitive perspective, CBT is effective because it corrects dysfunctional beliefs that underlie OCD symptoms (e.g., overestimates of threat) by presenting the patient with information that disconfirms these beliefs. Cognitive and psychoeducational interventions aim to modify such cognitions via a verbal-linguistic route, whereas exposure and response prevention accomplish the same goal experientially. CBT also helps patients gain self-efficacy by helping them to master their fears without having to rely on avoidance or safety behaviors.

Foa and Kozak (1986) have drawn attention to three indicators of change during exposure-based treatment of fear. First, physiological arousal and subjective fear must be evoked during exposure. Second, the fear responses gradually diminish during the exposure session (**within-session habituation**). Third, the initial fear response at the beginning of each exposure session declines across sessions (**between-sessions habituation**).

4.3   Efficacy and Prognosis

There is excellent scientific evidence of the effectiveness of CBT for OCD

Numerous uncontrolled and controlled studies evaluating the effectiveness of exposure-based CBT for OCD consistently show that patients who complete this treatment achieve clinically significant and durable improvement (Abramowitz, 1998). Average improvement rates are typically from 50% to 70% in these studies. A review of 12 trials ($N = 330$) indicated that 83% of patents were "responders" at posttreatment. In 16 studies reporting long-term outcome ($N = 376$; mean follow-up interval of 29 months), 76% were "responders" (Foa & Kozak, 1996). Meta-analytic studies (e.g., Abramowitz, 1996, 1997; Abramowitz, Franklin, & Foa, 2002) show that CBT produces consistently large effect sizes on measures of OCD, anxiety, and depression.

Recent randomized controlled studies have found exposure-based CBT superior to waiting list, progressive muscle relaxation, anxiety management training, pill placebo, and pharmacotherapy by clomipramine (e.g., Foa et al., 2005). These trials indicate that the effects of CBT are due to the specific cognitive and behavioral techniques (i.e., exposure and response prevention) over and above any effects of nonspecific factors common to all interventions, such as the therapeutic relationship. Moreover, the effects of CBT are not limited to highly selected research samples or to treatment as delivered in specialty clinics. **Effectiveness studies** conducted with nonresearch patients (e.g., Franklin, Abramowitz, Foa, Kozak, & Levitt, 2000) show that over 80% of patients who complete CBT achieve clinically significant improvement. Table 12 shows the results from studies of CBT in which the Y-BOCS was used as the primary

Table 12
Effects of Exposure-Based CBT in Trials Using the Y-BOCS

| | Y-BOCS total score | |
| | CBT group | Control group |
Study	M (SD)	M (SD)
Fals-Stewart et al. (1993)[1]		Relaxation
Pretest	20.2 (-)	19.9 (-)
Posttest	12.1 (-)	18.1 (-)
% reduction	40%	9%
Freeston et al. (1997)		Wait list
Pretest	25.1 (5.0)	21.2 (6.0)
Posttest	12.2 (9.6)	22.0 (6.0)
% reduction	51%	-4%
Lindsay et al. (1997)		Stress management
Pretest	28.7 (4.6)	24.4 (7.0)
Posttest	11.0 (3.8)	25.9 (5.8)
% reduction	62%	-6%
Franklin et al. (2000)		
Pretest	26.8 (4.9)	
Posttest	11.8 (7.3)	
% reduction	56%	
Warren & Thomas (2001)		
Pretest	23.0 (5.6)	
Posttest	11.6 (5.0)	
% reduction	50%	
Foa et al. (2005)		Pill placebo
Pretest	24.6 (4.8)	25.0 (4.0)
Posttest	11.0 (7.9)	22.2 (6.4)
% reduction	56%	11%

Y-BOCS = Yale-Brown Obsessive Compulsive Scale.
[1] Standard deviation not reported in the study.

outcome measure. While CBT is effective for most people with OCD, about 20% do not respond and about 25–30% drop out of therapy. Factors associated with poor outcome (e.g., severe depression) are discussed in Section 3.4.

4.4   Variations and Combinations of Methods

4.4.1   Variants of CBT Treatment Procedures

There is a relationship between treatment outcome and how CBT is delivered along three parameters. First, better short- and long-term outcome is achieved when treatment involves in-session exposure practice that is supervised by a therapist, as compared to when all exposure is performed by the patient as homework assignments. In fact, the number of hours of therapist-directed exposure is positively correlated with outcome. Second, combining situational and imaginal exposure is superior to situational exposure alone. Third, programs in which patients **completely** refrain from rituals during the treatment period (i.e., complete response prevention) produce superior immediate and long-term effects compared to those that involve only partial response prevention.

4.4.2   Combining Medication and CBT

Research suggests that medication neither adds to, nor detracts from, the effectiveness of CBT for OCD

The concurrent use of CBT and SRI medication for OCD is common in clinical settings. The available research indicates that whereas adding CBT to SRIs yields superior outcome compared to SRIs alone, adding SRIs neither improves nor attenuates the efficacy of CBT (e.g., Foa et al., 2005). Thus, CBT is an excellent augmentation strategy for individuals with OCD who remain symptomatic despite adequate trials of SRI medications.

4.5   Problems in Carrying out the Treatment

Table 13 lists common problems that arise during CBT for OCD. Suggestions for managing such obstacles are provided below.

4.5.1   Negative Reactions to the CBT Model

Some patients hold the belief that OCD symptoms are caused by a "chemical imbalance" and therefore "talk therapy" won't be helpful. Because such a view can lead to premature drop out, the therapist should openly discuss any doubts the patient has about the CBT model. Highlight that this model was developed to explain the **symptoms** of OCD, not necessarily its causes (therefore, the CBT approach is not incompatible with a biological approach). You might also point out that studies show CBT has effects on brain functioning.

Table 13
Common Obstacles in Cognitive-Behavior Therapy for OCD

- Negative reactions to the CBT model

- Nonadherence
  - Noncompliance with exposure instructions
  - Noncompliance with response prevention instructions
  - Continued use of avoidance and subtle rituals

- Arguments

- Therapist's inclination to challenge the obsession

- Cognitive therapy techniques that become rituals

- Unbearable anxiety levels during exposure

- Absence of anxiety during exposure

- Therapist discomfort with conducting exposure exercises

Common obstacles to the successful treatment of OCD

4.5.2   Nonadherence

The most common obstacle encountered in CBT for OCD is the patient's failure to follow through with treatment instructions. Many adherence problems can be circumvented by clarifying how exposure and response prevention reduce OCD symptoms. You should also actively involve the patient in the treatment planning process.

The degree of improvement obtained in CBT is often directly related to how well the patient adheres to the treatment instructions

Noncompliance with Exposure
If a patient refuses to complete exposure tasks (e.g., homework assignments), inquire as to why this is. Sometimes the problem can be addressed with simple problem solving (e.g., time management). Also, make sure the exposure task itself is a good match to the patient's obsessional fears. If not, the patient might perceive the exercise as irrelevant. If high levels of anxiety prompt refusal or "shortcuts" (e.g., subtle avoidance, rituals) during exposure, review the treatment rationale and use cognitive strategies to identify and address dysfunctional cognitions that underlie reluctance to confront the feared stimulus.

Refining the exposure hierarchy and adding intermediate items might be appropriate if the patient threatens to discontinue treatment. However, postponing exposures can reinforce avoidance. Thus, use this tactic only as a last resort. Instead, use Socratic questioning to create and amplify the discrepancy between nonadherence and the patient's goals. When nonadherence is perceived as conflicting with important personal goals (such as self-image, happiness, success), it increases motivation for change.

Noncompliance with Response Prevention
If the patient is deliberately concealing ritualistic behavior which was specifically prohibited by the treatment plan, explain the implications of this problem for treatment outcome in the following way:
Therapist: Your wife called to tell me that you changed your clothes several
    times last weekend after going in the basement. She felt I needed to be

aware of this because she was concerned that you weren't following the instructions we all agreed to at the beginning of therapy. We all agreed that if problems come up, you were going to get help from your wife instead of doing rituals. What happened?

If the patient makes a renewed agreement to adhere to the treatment instructions, the issue can be dropped. However, if repeated infractions occur, remind the patient of the rationale for response prevention and raise the possibility of suspending treatment. For example:

Therapist: It seems that right now you aren't able to stop your rituals as we had agreed at the beginning of treatment. Remember that each time you do a ritual you are preventing yourself from learning that your distress would have declined on its own—even without the ritual. If you cannot follow the treatment rules, we should talk about whether now is the right time for you to be doing this kind of treatment.

Continued Use of Avoidance and Subtle Rituals

Perhaps unintentionally, patients sometimes adopt covert tactics for avoiding or neutralizing obsessional distress once they are told to stop their overt rituals. Examples include the use of brief actions (e.g., quickly wiping hands instead of washing) or mental rituals (e.g., instead of asking for reassurance). Although the patient might not realize that he or she is doing anything wrong, such safety behaviors are functionally equivalent to rituals: they interfere with habituation and prevent cognitive change. Therefore, these behaviors must be dropped. If the patient reports that anxiety is not declining with repeated exposures, inquire about such "mini rituals." For example, "Now that you've stopped your compulsive rituals, are you doing any little things to relieve anxiety?"

4.5.3   Arguments

Some patients become argumentative about the "strictness" of response prevention rules or the "dangerousness" of exposure tasks. You should resist the urge to lecture the patient, and instead use Socratic methods so that the belief-altering information is generated by the patient him or herself.

It is important to avoid arguing with patients about the treatment instructions

In the example below, the patient argues that speaking **one more time** with an infectious disease expert (Dr. B) would terminate his need for reassurance about the risk of catching AIDS from public restrooms:

Clinical Vignette

The Use of Socratic Dialog to Address Patient Arguments

Patient: I just *have* to ask Dr. B one more question about catching AIDS from public toilets. I can't go on without asking.

Therapist: I understand that you are anxious about this. Let's talk about that decision, though. You know that would be a violation of response prevention.

Patient: But I need to know. I might have put myself at risk of catching AIDS. You don't understand. I'm so worried.

Therapist:	What has Dr. B told you in the past when you've asked her about these kinds of situations?
Patient:	That I'm not likely to catch AIDS that way. But this time it's different. I *really* feel like I could have AIDS. Please, just one more time. I have to ask her.
Therapist:	Oh, so, each time you've asked Dr. B about AIDS, she tells you that you have nothing to worry about. That's interesting. What do you think she'll say to you this time?
Patient:	I hadn't thought about it that way before. You're right. She'll probably tell me the same thing.
Therapist:	OK, so if you already know what she'll say, would you agree that it would be more helpful for you to learn new ways of reducing your anxiety rather than asking Dr. B. for reassurances whenever you have obsessions about AIDS? We've discussed how the reassurance-seeking only makes OCD stronger.
Patient:	Yes. I see what you mean.

If discussions about the risks associated with exposure tasks become combative, summarize the discussion and agree with the patient that his or her assertion **could** be correct; but that rather than taking anything for granted, it is better to closely examine the facts (e.g., using exposure). Do your best to refrain from debates over probability or the degree of risk. Such arguments

Clinical Pearl
When the Patient Argues

When a patient becomes argumentative (e.g., during exposure), it might indicate a rising level of distress. Instead of engaging in arguments about risk or "what is normal," the best strategy is to use conflict resolution strategies, such as the "broken record technique" (refrain from escalating the argument by re-stating your original point) or "turning the tables" (identify the problem and ask the patient what he or she would do to resolve it). Of course, set your limits and know how far it is reasonable to bend the therapy instructions. Statements such as the following might also be helpful:

What to do if the patient is argumentative

- You are here in treatment for yourself—not for me. So, I won't argue or debate with you. Doing the treatment is entirely your choice. You stand to get better by trying these exercises and enduring the short-term anxiety. But you are also the one who has to live with the OCD symptoms if you choose not to do the therapy.

- Remember that we both agreed on the treatment plan. I expect you to hold up your end of the bargain.

- I agree with you that there is *some* risk involved; but it is not *high* risk. The goal of treatment is to weaken your anxiety about situations where it is impossible to have a complete guarantee of safety.

- I realize *most* people wouldn't go out of their way to do what I am asking you to do. But the therapy isn't about what people *usually* do. These tasks are designed to help you learn to manage acceptable levels of risk and uncertainty.

- I know this is a difficult decision for you. Yet, if you are going to get over OCD, you have to confront your uncertainty and find out that the risk is low.

reinforce the patient's OCD habits of spending too much time thinking about these issues and they amount to little more than a playing out of the patient's fruitless (ritualistic) attempts to gain reassurance. Moreover, when patients perceive that the therapist is frustrated, angry, or coercive (e.g., "you can't **make** me do this"), they lose motivation. Instead, step back and recognize that the decision to engage in treatment is a difficult one.

4.5.4   Therapist's Inclination to Challenge the Obsession

Therapists occasionally fall into the trap of challenging the logic of patients' obsessional thoughts per se (e.g., "the impulse to attack an elderly person") rather than challenging the patient's faulty beliefs **about** the obsessions. The vignette below highlights the distinction between these two approaches:

Clinical Vignette
Challenging Obsessions

Example 1: Challenging the obsession

Therapist: Which intrusive thoughts have been particular problems for you this week?

Patient: Every time I am around my grandfather, I get these terrible images of attacking him. He's such an old man and I love him very much. But I can't stop thinking about beating him.

Therapist: Let's look at the evidence. What do you think the likelihood is that you will beat your grandfather?

Patient: Pretty low. I've never done it before even though I've thought about it a lot.

Example 2: Challenging faulty appraisals and beliefs

Therapist: Which intrusive thoughts have been particular problems for you this week?

Patient: Every time I am around my grandfather, I get these terrible images of attacking him. He's such an old man and I love him very much. But I can't stop thinking about beating him.

Therapist: When these kinds of thoughts come up, how do you interpret them? What do they mean to you?

Patient: They mean that I am a terrible person deep down. I mean who the hell thinks of killing their own grandfather? I need to be careful that I don't do anything awful, so I avoid him.

Therapist: Let's look more closely at your beliefs about these unwanted thoughts. Where is the evidence that because you have violent thoughts, you're really a violent person? What do we know about who has violent thoughts?

Patient: Well, once in a while everyone has bad thoughts like I do. So, maybe the thoughts aren't as troubling as I'm thinking they are.

Intuitively, the obsession itself seems like a good target for cognitive techniques because it is a cognitive event and it is irrational. Yet, most patients already recognize the irrationality of their obsessions. So, direct challenges will have only a transient therapeutic effect. Moreover, such challenges could turn into reassurance-seeking strategies used to neutralize the obsession. In contrast, challenging the **appraisal** of the obsession gives the patient new information that is different from reassurance.

4.5.5 When Cognitive Interventions Become Rituals

Some patients convert discussions about mistaken beliefs into reassurance seeking rituals. For example, one patient ritualistically repeated (3 times perfectly) the phrase "obsessional thoughts are normal" to reduce anxiety associated with his unwanted homosexual images. Others become preoccupied with identifying the **perfect** rational belief that **best** reassures them that feared consequences are impossible. The best way to sidestep these problems is to avoid giving the patient a **guarantee** of safety.

As a general rule, if the patient uses psychoeducational information in a stereotypic way, or requires increasing clarification to reduce distress, the material is probably being used as a ritual. In contrast, healthy use of cognitive techniques allows the patient to generate (him- or herself) new interpretations of obsessional stimuli that lead to acting appropriately during exposure.

4.5.6 Unbearable Anxiety Levels During Exposure

If the patient becomes extremely anxious or emotional during an exposure, the task might be too difficult. In such cases, the exercise should be stopped and you should assess the underlying cognitions. What was it that was so anxiety-provoking? A less difficult task can be used instead. If the patient is concerned that therapy isn't working because anxiety doesn't subside, emphasize that treatment requires continued practice. Point out that the patient took an important step simply by choosing to enter the feared situation in the first place.

4.5.7 Absence of Anxiety During Exposure

If the patient reports little or no distress during exposure, it could mean one of three things. First, the situation might no longer evoke anxiety. That is, the patient's expectations about danger have been modified. This is most likely to occur toward the end of treatment. In such cases, you can skip to another hierarchy item. A second explanation is that you have not incorporated the main anxiety-evoking aspect(s) of the feared situation into the exposure task. To troubleshoot, ask the patient why the exercise does not evoke anxiety, or how it could be made more anxiety evoking. A third possibility is that the patient has nullified the exposure with cognitive avoidance or safety-seeking behavior. For example, before conducting a driving exposure, one patient called her neighbors to "warn" them to closely watch their children during the time she would be driving through the neighborhood streets. This absolved her of the responsibility for harm and therefore she did not become anxious during the driving exposure. The use of such strategies indicates a problem in understanding the treatment rationale and must be addressed.

4.5.8   Therapist Discomfort with Conducting Exposure Exercises

If you are not accustomed to using exposure techniques, you might feel apprehensive about asking patients with OCD to purposely confront stimuli that will evoke discomfort. Recall, however, that the beneficial effects of CBT are well-documented. Reducing OCD in the long-run requires evocation of temporary anxiety. Also, recall that exposure helps patients learn that their feared situations and thoughts do not objectively pose a high risk of threat. Response prevention helps the patient learn that time-consuming and embarrassing rituals are not necessary to prevent feared outcomes. In fact, when the rationale for CBT is clear and the treatment plan is set up collaboratively, doing this treatment prompts a supportive and highly rewarding working relationship which helps the patient make considerable and long-lasting progress.

5

Case Vignettes

This chapter presents examples of fear hierarchies and treatment plans (session-by-session descriptions of situational and imaginal exposure tasks) for common presentations of OCD. CBT in each of these four cases resulted in marked reductions in symptoms, dramatic diminution in ritualistic behaviors, and significant enhancement of each patient's ability to cope with distressing and intrusive thoughts. You can use these vignettes as templates for building CBT programs for your patients.

Case 1: Contamination Symptoms

Kristi, a 36-year-old hotel manager, feared contracting the herpes virus. She avoided public bathrooms and contact with surfaces such as door handles and garbage cans. She also avoided contact with other people and their belongings (pens, office telephones, etc.). Bodily waste and secretions such as urine, feces, and sweat also evoked obsessive fear. Kristi washed her hands over 50 times each day and often showered and changed her clothes multiple times to reduce her fears of contamination.

Kristi's fear hierarchy was as follows:

Hierarchy Item	SUDS
Door handles and hand rails	45
Images of "herpes germs"	55
Shaking hands with others	65
Public telephones	70
Images of getting cold sores from herpes	70
Garbage cans	75
Sweat	80
Images of becoming terribly ill	80
Public bathrooms	85
Urine	90
Feces	95

Kristi's response prevention plan was as follows:
- No contact with water except for one 10-minute shower and one 2-minute tooth brushing each day. Immediately after contact with water, she was to re-expose herself to stimuli from the fear hierarchy.
- No changing of clothes after dressing for the day.

During the first exposure session, Kristi and the therapist walked through the clinic and touched door handles and hand rails, maintaining contact with each for a period of several minutes. In the therapist's office, Kristi described her intrusive images of "herpes germs" crawling all over her body into a tape recorder and listened to the tape repeatedly for imaginal exposure. Between sessions, she conducted daily self-exposures to door handles and other surfaces in places that she had been avoiding, such as work and certain stores. She also practiced imaginal exposure using the recorded material.

At the second session, Kristi practiced shaking hands with clinic staff (strangers). She also touched public telephones, concentrating on the receiver since she was concerned about germs from other peoples' mouths. Imaginal exposure involved distressing images of cold sores, uncertainty about where people might have put their hands, and who might have used the telephones she touched. Between sessions, she practiced shaking hands and touching public phones, especially before eating.

During the third session, Kristi practiced touching garbage cans, especially those in public areas such as malls. Imaginal exposure to images of germs was continued, and Kristi practiced eating with her hands immediately after contact with trash cans. She repeated these and similar exercises each day between the third and fourth sessions.

At the fourth session, exposure to sweat was conducted by having Kristi run in place and then put one hand under her arm and the other inside her shoe. Imaginal exposure involved thinking of becoming ill from "sweat germs." Kristi kept a soiled sock in her pocket between sessions. She handled the sock each time before she ate.

Public bathrooms were the focus of session 5. Kristi confronted bathroom door handles, sink faucets, and soap dispensers by maintaining contact with these items for several minutes. She confronted toilets by sitting next to the bowl and touching the flusher and seat. For practice between sessions, she was instructed to sit on public toilets in various places she had been avoiding (e.g., mall bathrooms). Imaginal exposure included images of germs, cold sores, and of becoming ill.

Session 6 again involved a supervised public bathroom exposure. After touching the toilet, urine was confronted by having Kristi hold a paper towel dampened with a few drops of her own urine specimen collected earlier that day. Between sessions, Kristi carried the paper towel in her pocket and frequently touched it to her hands.

At session 7, exposure included public toilets and urine, with the introduction of feces (a piece of toilet paper lightly soiled with her own excrement). Kristi was instructed to practice with feces, urine, and toilet seats between sessions.

Sessions 8 through 16 included repeated exposures to public bathrooms, urine, and feces—which provoked the greatest discomfort. She practiced eating and touching personal items (e.g., her purse) immediately following these exposures. Imaginal exposure to distressing thoughts and periodic contact with lesser contaminants was continued. Kristi was also encouraged to contaminate additional personal items at home and at work.

Case 2: Harming Symptoms

Steve, a 33-year-old real estate agent, performed checking rituals that were precipitated by thoughts that he could become responsible for injury to others and their property. If he saw a fire truck or ambulance, he worried that perhaps he had started a fire or caused an accident without realizing it. He watched the TV news, scoured the newspapers, and even checked with police to ensure he had not caused such disasters. He often returned to houses he had shown to potential buyers to make sure all appliances were off and doors locked. After his wife and children went to sleep each night, Steve spent hours checking the electrical appliances, door locks, windows, and water faucets in his home; and the parking brake of his car.

Steve's fear hierarchy was as follows:

Hierarchy Item	SUDS
Turn light switch on and off	45
Images of fires	50
Open and close window	55
Open/close car door and enable/disable parking break	65
Images of accidents	70
Turn appliances on and off	75
Turn water faucet on and off	80

Steve's response prevention plan was as follows:
- No checking doors, windows, appliances, the car,
- No seeking reassurance by asking other people (e.g., family, police officers) about disasters.
- No returning to other homes to check for safety.
- No watching the news or reading the local section of the newspaper to look for possible disasters.

The first treatment session began at Steve's home where all of the lights were first turned on. Then, Steve quickly went through the house (unsupervised by the therapist) and turned the lights off without checking (no one else was home at the time). He then left the house and drove away. For imaginal exposure, Steve practiced thinking about house fires that might have started from leaving lights on in the house. Each day between the first and second sessions, Steve practiced this exercise after his wife and children had left the house for the day.

The second session was also held at Steve's house. Exposure involved opening and closing windows on the ground floor without checking, followed by quickly leaving the house. Again, between sessions, Steve practiced this exercise while his family was out for the day.

At the third session, situational exposure involved Steve and the therapist driving around the block in Steve's car, rolling down the windows, and unlocking the doors. After arriving back at the clinic, Steve turned off the car engine, applied the parking break, rolled up the windows, and locked the car doors before quickly evacuating the car and, without checking, walking into the clinic building. Secondary imaginal exposure to thoughts about the feared consequences of leaving the parking break off, windows down, and doors unlocked, was conducted once in the therapist's office. Steve practiced similar exercises each day between sessions 3 and 4. During session 4, primary imaginal exposure to thoughts of unknowingly causing accidents was added to the situational exposure. Between sessions, Steve practiced these tasks.

Sessions 5 and 6 took place in Steve's home. During session 5, in addition to windows and lights, exposure included practice turning appliances on and off and then leaving the house without checking. Steve conducted secondary imaginal exposure to images of house fires for which he was responsible because of the failure to check. At session 6, turning water faucets on and off was added to the exposure tasks. Between sessions, assignments included daily repetitions of these same exercises.

Sessions 7 through 16 focused on conducting exposures in different contexts. For example, Steve and the therapist visited several homes for sale. Steve practiced turning lights and appliances on and off in each home, and then leaving the home and conducting imaginal exposures to thoughts of causing fires. Between sessions, he also practiced turning lights and appliances on and off, and unlocking and locking doors and windows, before going to bed in his own home.

Case 3: Incompleteness Symptoms

Jill, a 26-year-old woman who lived with her parents, engaged in ordering, arranging, and balancing rituals triggered by distressing obsessional thoughts of "imperfection" and "imbalance." Activities such as completing paperwork often took hours because Jill had to painstakingly make sure that letters were formed correctly and "perfectly." Items in the house had to be arranged in certain ways and Jill had to ensure that such order was maintained. Her most pervasive symptoms focused on left-right balance. For example, if she used her **right** hand to open a door or to grab something (e.g., from the refrigerator), she felt an urge to repeat the behavior using her **left** hand (and vice versa) to achieve balance. These symptoms limited Jill's ability to function to the point that on many days she was unable to leave the house.

Jill's fear hierarchy was as follows:

Hierarchy Item	SUDS
Write letters "Imperfectly"	40
Write imperfectly in checkbook	55
Leave items in the family room "out of order"	67
Leave items in own room "out of order"	75
Say, write, and hear the word "left" without the word "right"	75
"Notice" left-right imbalance	80
Touch items on right (or left) side only	85

Jill's response prevention plan was as follows:
• No re-writing.
• No ordering/arranging

- No attempts to achieve left-right balance visually, verbally, motorically, or otherwise

At session 1, Jill practiced writing letters imperfectly (e.g., sloppily); first on blank pieces of paper, then on notes she was sending to others, and finally on paperwork such as financial statements. This was also practiced between sessions.

Session 2 began with more practice writing imperfectly, this time culminating with Jill filling out her checkbook imperfectly. Homework exposure involved writing imperfectly (e.g., sloppily)

At the third and fourth sessions, Jill practiced rearranging items in the therapist's office so that they were "not balanced." For example, she tilted the therapist's picture frames slightly to the right and shifted books on the bookshelves to the right. Jill's homework assignments involved gradually rearranging items in her own home so that they seemed "out of order." This began with items in the living room and eventually involved items in her bedroom. Jill was instructed to remind herself that these items were "out of order," but to also refrain from urges to re-arrange them the "correct" way.

The fifth session involved confrontation with the word "left" in the absence of the word "right." Jill practiced saying "left" and even writing it on the back of both of her hands. Homework exposure involved further exposure to "left." She also kept a piece of paper with this word in her pocket at all times.

Session 6 involved continued exposure to the word "left," as well as to purposely noticing left-right imbalance and not performing any "balancing" rituals. Jill and therapist walked though the clinic and purposely noticed unevenness (e.g., elevator buttons on the right side of the elevator, the fact that more people were sitting on the right side of the waiting room than on the left side). Jill also purposely brushed against objects such as walls and desks on her left or her right side without "balancing" this out. She completed similar exposures between sessions. In addition, she was instructed to leave her belt buckle slightly off center (facing left) and to tie her left shoe noticeably more tightly than her right shoe.

Sessions 7 through 16 involved repeated exposure to left-right imbalance in various contexts. For example, Jill created this imbalance in her bedroom and encouraged her parents to do the same in various parts of the house.

Case 4: Unacceptable Thoughts

Matt, was a devoutly religious 25-year-old married (heterosexual) graduate student with recurrent unwanted homosexual thoughts and images. These obsessions were triggered by hearing certain words (e.g., "penis") and by the sight of certain men—especially Matt's friend, Todd. Matt was avoiding spending time with his male friends and had stopped going to the gym, where he might see other men undressed in the locker room. He was also avoiding sexual intercourse with his wife because the homosexual thoughts had once occurred during sex. Matt feared that the frequency and intensity of his obsessions indicated that he was "turning gay"; something that was strictly forbidden from his religious viewpoint. When the thoughts came to mind, he tried to "analyze" their meaning and often "tested" himself by looking at (or thinking of) attractive women to reassure himself that he was still heterosexual. These mental rituals sometimes lasted for hours each day. Matt also prayed ritualistically that he was not becoming gay.

Matt's fear hierarchy was as follows:

Hierarchy Item	SUDS
Words ("gay" "penis" "homosexual")	55
Pictures of handsome men (models)	65
Pictures of Todd	70
Mental images of Todd's penis	75
Gym/locker room	75
Homoerotic pornography	80
Images of having sex with other men	90
Sexual intercourse with wife	95

Matt's response prevention plan was as follows:
- No mental analyzing of the meaning of thoughts
- No "testing" for reassurance of heterosexuality
- Refrain from any prayers about intrusive thoughts

During the first exposure session, Matt practiced saying the words "penis," "gay," "homosexual," "anal sex," and "blow job," which were anxiety-provoking for him. He also repeatedly wrote these words on sheets of paper that he kept in his wallet. Homework practice included repeating these exercises daily.

At session 2, Matt viewed pictures of attractive men by looking through fitness and fashion magazines. He was instructed to discuss of how good-looking he thought these men were. He also took the magazines home so that he could repeat this task between sessions.

During the third session, Matt looked at pictures of his friend Todd for exposure. For imaginal exposure, he visualized what Todd would look like nude, including having images of his penis. Matt was instructed to repeat this exercise each day between sessions, and to expose himself imaginally to the doubts about his sexual preference that this exercise evoked.

Exposure to watching men in the fitness club during the fourth exposure session was engineered as follows: Matt and the therapist met at the gym during the busiest time of day. They stood on the balcony above the weight room and the therapist instructed Matt to notice and remark about men's physiques. Matt went into the men's locker room and struck up a conversation with a man who was undressed and preparing to take a shower. During the brief conversation, Matt surreptitiously noticed the man's naked body, as the therapist had coached him to do. Matt repeated this exposure several times between sessions.

During the fifth session, Matt viewed explicit pornographic images and films of men engaged in autoerotic and homosexual activity. He repeated these exposures between sessions.

At the sixth session, Matt again practiced viewing images of homosexual activity. To confront images of having sex with other men, he wrote a story describing himself engaged in such activities with his friend, Todd. Matt was instructed to vividly describe the events. He wrote similar stories between sessions.

During sessions 7 to 16, Matt practiced viewing more homoerotic pornography and writing additional stories about sexual encounters between himself and other men. These "fantasies" were varied according to what evoked greater distress; for example, the use of more intense and graphic imagery. Matt also was instructed to resume intercourse with his wife and to resist urges to dismiss any intrusive homosexual thoughts that came to mind.

6

Further Reading

This section includes key references to literature where the practitioner can find further details or background information. Each reference includes a brief (2–5 lines) annotation.

Abramowitz, J. (2006). *Understanding and treating obsessive-compulsive disorder: A cognitive-behavioral approach.* New York: Lawrence Erlbaum Associates.
Presents didactic material on the clinical features and psychological theories of OCD. Also contains a manual for cognitive-behavioral assessment and treatment.
Abramowitz, J., Franklin, M., & Cahill, S. (2003). Approaches to common obstacles in the exposure-based treatment of obsessive-compulsive disorder. *Cognitive and Behavioral Practice, 10,* 14–22. This article discusses a number of problems that can arise during CBT for OCD. Case examples are presented and suggestions for managing these problems are described.
Clark, D. (2004). *Cognitive-behavioral therapy for OCD.* New York: Guilford. This book provides the reader with an in-depth review of OCD symptoms and theories, emphasizing cognitive theory. The use of cognitive therapy techniques for OCD is also outlined in manual form.

7

References

Abramowitz, J. (1998). Does cognitive-behavioral therapy cure obsessive-compulsive disorder? A Meta-analytic evaluation of clinical significance. *Behavior Therapy, 29*, 339–355.

Abramowitz, J. S. (1996). Variants of exposure and response prevention in the treatment of obsessive-compulsive disorder: A meta-analysis. *Behavior Therapy, 27*, 583–600.

Abramowitz, J. S. (1997). Effectiveness of psychological and pharmacological treatments for obsessive-compulsive disorder: A quantitative review. *Journal of Consulting and Clinical Psychology, 65*(1), 44–52.

Abramowitz, J. S., Franklin, M. E., & Foa, E. B. (2002). Empirical status of cognitive-behavioral therapy for obsessive-compulsive disorder: A meta-analytic review. *Romanian Journal of Cognitive and Behavioral Psychotherapies, 2*(2), 89–104.

Abramowitz, J. S., Franklin, M. E., Schwartz, S. A., & Furr, J. M. (2003). Symptom presentation and outcome of cognitive-behavioral therapy for obsessive-compulsive disorder. *Journal of Consulting and Clinical Psychology, 71*(6), 1049–1057.

American Psychiatric Association (2000). *Diagnostic and statistical manual of mental disorders (4th ed., Text revision) (DSM-IV-TR)*. Washington, DC: Author.

Beck, A. T., Epstein, N., Brown, G. & Steer, R.A. (1988). An inventory for measuring clinical anxiety: psychometric properties. *Journal of Consulting and Clinical Psychology, 56*, 893–897.

Beck, A. T., Ward, C. H., Medelsohn, M., Mock, J., & Erlbaugh, J. (1961). An inventory for measuring depression. *Archives of General Psychiatry, 4*, 561–571.

Crino, R. D., & Andrews, G. (1996a). Obsessive-compulsive disorder and Axis I comorbidity. *Journal of Anxiety Disorders, 10*(1), 37–46.

Crino, R. D., & Andrews, G. (1996b). Personality disorder in obsessive compulsive disorder: A controlled study. *Journal of Psychiatric Research, 30*(1), 29–38.

Di Nardo, P., Brown, T., & Barlow, D. H. (1994). *Anxiety Disorders Interview Schedule for DSM-IV: Lifetime Version (ADIS-IV-LV)*. San Antonio, TX: The Psychological Corporation.

Eisen, J. L., Phillips, K. A., Baer, L., Beer, D. A., Atala, K. D., & Rasmussen, S. A. (1998). The Brown Assessment of Beliefs Scale: Reliability and validity. *American Journal of Psychiatry, 155*(1), 102–108.

First, M. B., Spitzer, R. L., Gibbon, M., & Williams, J. (2002). *Structured Clinical Interview for the DSM-IV Axis 1 Disorders*. New York, NY: Biometrics Research Department, new York State Psychiatric Institute.

Foa, E., & Kozak, M. (1986). Emotional processing of fear: exposure to corrective information. *Psychological Bulletin, 99*, 20–35.

Foa, E., Liebowitz, M. R., Kozak, M. J., Davies, S., Campeas, R., Franklin, M. E., et al. (2005). Randomized, placebo-controlled trial of exposure and ritual prevention, clomipramine, and their combination in the treatment of obsessive-compulsive disorder. *American Journal of Psychiatry, 162*, 151–161.

Foa, E. B., Huppert, J. D., Leiberg, S., Langner, R., Kichic, R., Hajcak, G., & Salkovskis, P. M. (2002). The Obsessive-Compulsive Inventory: Development and validation of a short version. *Psychological Assessment, 14*, 485–496.

Foa, E. B., & Kozak, M. J. (1996). Psychological treatment for obsessive-compulsive disorder. In M. R. Mavissakalian & R. F. Prien (Eds.), *Long-term treatments of anxiety disorders* (pp. 285–309). Washington, DC: American Psychiatric Press, Inc.

Franklin, M. E., Abramowitz, J. S., Foa, E. B., Kozak, M. J., & Levitt, J. T. (2000). Effectiveness of exposure and ritual prevention for obsessive-compulsive disorder: Randomized compared with nonrandomized samples. *Journal of Consulting and Clinical Psychology, 68*(4), 594–602.

Frost, R. O., & Steketee, S. (2002). *Cognitive approaches to obsessions and compulsions: Theory, assessment, and treatment.* Oxford: Elsevier.

Goodman, W. K., Price, L. H., Rasmussen, S. A., Mazure, C., Delgado, P., Heninger, G. R., et al. (1989). The Yale-Brown Obsessive Compulsive Scale: validity. *Archives of General Psychiatry, 46*, 1012–1016.

Goodman, W. K., Price, L. H., Rasmussen, S. A., Mazure, C., Fleischmann, R. L., Hill, C. L., et al. (1989). The Yale-Brown Obsessive Compulsive Scale: Development, use, and reliability. *Archives of General Psychiatry, 46*, 1006–1011.

Gross, R. C., Sasson, Y., Chorpa, M., & Zohar, J. (1998). Biological models of obsessive-compulsive disorder: The serotonin hypothesis. In R. P. Swinson, M. Antony, S. Rachman & M. Richter (Eds.), *Obsessive-compulsive disorder: Theory, research, and treatment* (pp. 141–153). New York: Guilford.

Hamilton, M. (1960). A rating scale for depression. *Journal of Neurological and Neurosurgical Psychiatry, 18*, 315–319.

Hiss, H., Foa, E. B., & Kozak, M. J. (1994). Relapse prevention program for treatment of obsessive-compulsive disorder. *Journal of Consulting and Clinical Psychology, 62*(4), 801–808.

Karno, M., Golding, J., Sorenson, S., & Burnam, A. (1988). The epidemiology of obsessive-compulsive disorder in five US communities. *Archives of General Psychiatry, 45*, 1094–1099.

Kozak, M. J., & Coles, M. E. (2005). Treatment of obsessive-compulsive disorder: Unleashing the power of exposure. In J. S. Abramowitz & A. C. Houts (Eds.), *Concepts and controversies in obsessive-compulsive disorder* (pp. 283–304). New York: Springer.

McKay, D., Abramowitz, J. S., Calamari, J. E., Kyrios, M., Radomsky, A. S., Sookman, D., et al. (2004). A critical evaluation of obsessive-compulsive disorder subtypes: Symptoms versus mechanisms. *Clinical Psychology Review, 24*, 283–313.

McNally, R. J. (2000). Information-processing abnormalities in obsessive-compulsive disorder. In W. K. Goodman, M. V. Rudorfer, & J. D. Maser (Eds.), *Obsessive-compulsive disorder: Contemporary issues in treatment.* (pp. 105–116). Mahwah, NJ: Lawrence Erlbaum Associates, Inc.

Mowrer, O. (1960). *Learning theory and behavior.* New York: Wiley.

Rachman, S., & Hodgson, R. (1980). *Obsessions and compulsions.* Englewood Cliffs, NJ: Prentice Hall.

Saxena, S., Bota, R. G., & Brody, A. L. (2001). Brain-behavior relationships in obsessive-compulsive disorder. *Seminars in Clinical Neuropsychiatry, 6*, 82–101.

Shafran, R. (2005). Cognitive-behavioral models of OCD. In J. S. Abramowitz & A. C. Houts (Eds.), *Concepts and controversies in obsessive-compulsive disorder.* New York: Springer.

Williams, K., Chambless, D. L., & Steketee, G. (1998). Behavioral treatment of obsessive-compulsive disorder in African Americans: Clinical issues. *Journal of Behavior Therapy & Experimental Psychiatry, 29*(2), 163–170.

8

Appendix: Tools and Resources

This appendix contains tools and resources that therapists can copy and give to patients. These include a functional assessment form, a fear hierarchy form, a self-monitoring form, a hand-out on intrusive thoughts, guidelines for successful exposure, and an exposure practice form.

Functional Assessment of OCD Symptoms

Date:

Patient Name: _____   Present age: _____

Date of birth: _____   Duration of symptoms:_____

Educational level: _____

Obsessional Stimuli

- **External triggers of obsessions** (people, places, things, and situations that evoke anxiety; e.g., mold, leaving home, "13")

_____

_____

_____

_____

_____

_____

_____

- **Obsessional thoughts, impulses, images, doubts** (e.g., "God is dead", images of germs, impulse to harm, doubts about fires)

_____

_____

_____

_____

_____

_____

_____

_____

Hogrefe & Huber Publishers

Cognitive Features

- **Feared consequences of exposure to obsessional triggers** (e.g., "I will get sick if I don't wash my hands")

_____

_____

_____

_____

_____

_____

_____

_____

- **Catastrophic interpretations of intrusive thoughts** (e.g., "thinking about it is the same as doing it")

_____

_____

_____

_____

_____

_____

_____

_____

- **Fears of long-term anxiety/discomfort** ("I will be anxious forever unless I ritualize")

_____

_____

_____

_____

_____

_____

_____

From: J.S. Abramowitz: _Obsessive-Compulsive Disorder_   Hogrefe & Huber Publishers

Responses to Obsessional Distress (Safety-Seeking Behaviors)

- **Passive avoidance** (identify its relationship to obsessional fear; e.g., avoids old buildings due to fears of asbestos)

_____

_____

_____

_____

_____

_____

_____

_____

- **Overt compulsive rituals** (identify relationships to obsessional fear; e.g., checks the door to prevent burglary; reassurance seeking)

_____

_____

_____

_____

_____

_____

_____

_____

- **Mental rituals, covert neutralizing strategies** (e.g., thought suppression, mental reviewing, using positive images; identify relationships to obsessional fear)

_____

_____

_____

_____

_____

_____

_____

_____

From: J.S. Abramowitz: _Obsessive-Compulsive Disorder_   Hogrefe & Huber Publishers

Self-Monitoring of OCD Symptoms

Ritual 1: _____   Ritual 2: _____

Date	Time	What triggered the ritual? (brief summary of situation or thought)	Time spent with ritual 1	2

Hogrefe & Huber Publishers

Everyone Has Intrusive Thoughts

In obsessive-compulsive disorder (OCD), *obsessions* are defined as unwanted intrusive thoughts, ideas, or images that trigger anxiety, fear, or discomfort. The content of obsessions is often senseless or bizarre. The themes of obsessions often concern harm, violence, aggression, sex, religion, mistakes, physical appearance, germs, diseases, need for exactness, among other things. Because obsessions evoke anxiety and distress, people usually try to resist, stop, or control these intrusive thoughts. But this often doesn't work, or perhaps it works only for a short time. Then, the thought returns and can develop a "life of its own."

What many people do not realize is that practically everyone experiences unwanted intrusive thoughts (whether or not they have OCD). These sorts of thoughts are part of normal human thinking. The focus of this handout is to teach you that the unpleasant, distressing, repugnant, bizarre, and senseless obsessional thoughts that you are experiencing are not at all dangerous or abnormal.

Intrusive Thoughts Are Normal

Everyone knows the experience of senseless intrusive thoughts. Whether it is a daydream about winning the lottery, a frightening image of harm or danger, or a senseless doubt that is completely opposite of how you usually think, all humans have senseless and unwanted thoughts. You may be surprised to learn that even the kinds of intrusive, upsetting, unacceptable unwanted thoughts that resemble obsessions in OCD are experienced by just about everyone in the world. That is, *people without OCD experience the same kinds of unwanted and intrusive thoughts as do people with OCD*. The list below shows examples of intrusive thoughts reported by people *without* OCD:

- Thought of jumping off the bridge onto the highway below
- Thought of running car off the road or onto oncoming traffic
- Thought of poking something into my eyes
- Impulse to jump onto the tracks as the train comes into the station
- Image of hurting or killing a loved one
- Idea of doing something mean towards an elderly person or a small baby
- Thought of wishing that a person would die
- Impulse to run over a pedestrian who walks too slow
- Impulse to slap someone who talks too much
- Thought of something going terribly wrong because of my error
- Thought of having an accident while driving with children
- Thought of accidentally hitting someone with my car
- Image of loved one being injured or killed
- Thought of receiving news of a close relative's death
- Idea that other people might think that I am guilty of stealing
- Thought of being poked in eye by an umbrella

From: J.S. Abramowitz: *Obsessive-Compulsive Disorder*   Hogrefe & Huber Publishers

- Thought of being trapped in a car under water
- Thought of catching diseases from various places such as a toilet
- Thought of dirt that is always on my hand
- Thought of contracting a disease from contact with person
- Urge to insult friend for no apparent reason
- Image of screaming at my relatives
- Impulse to say something nasty or inappropriate to someone
- Impulse to do something shameful or terrible
- Thought that I left door unlocked
- Thought of my house getting broken into while I'm not home
- Thought that I left appliance on and cause a fire
- Thought of sexually molesting young children
- Thought that my house burned and I lost everything I own
- Thought that I have left car unlocked
- Thought that is contrary to my moral and religious beliefs
- Hoping someone doesn't succeed
- Thoughts of smashing a table full of crafts made of glass
- Thoughts of acts of violence in sex
- Sexual impulse toward attractive females
- Thought of "unnatural" sexual acts
- Image of a penis
- Image of grandparents having sex
- Thought about objects not arranged perfectly

Why do all people get these kinds of intrusive thoughts? This is probably because as humans we have highly developed and creative brains that can imagine all kinds of scenarios—some more pleasant than others. Sometimes, our "thought generator" produces thoughts about danger even though there may not be any real threat present. Humans have many thoughts while awake and during sleep, so it would be expected that our brains will sometimes create bizarre or senseless thoughts ("mental noise"). Often, such thoughts are triggered by actual situations, such as the sight of a knife, bathroom, driving, or a religious icon.

Scientists have conducted many studies on unwanted intrusive thoughts in people with and without OCD. All of these studies confirm that people with and without OCD have the same kinds of intrusive thoughts. In the most well-known study, researchers asked people with OCD and people without OCD to list some of their unpleasant unwanted thoughts. The lists (which resembled the list of thoughts shown above) were then given to psychologists and psychiatrists who were asked to say which thought came from people with and without OCD. But most of the time, even these professionals could not tell whether the thought was a clinical obsession from someone with OCD or a "normal obsession" from a nonOCD person.

This study (and several others like it) confirms that people with OCD do not have something abnormal in their brain that causes them to have terrible, senseless, or immoral obsessive thoughts. Instead, obsessions in OCD (even the most unacceptable, disgusting, violent, depraved thoughts and images) develop from entirely normal experiences as we will explore in this handout.

From: J.S. Abramowitz: *Obsessive-Compulsive Disorder*   Hogrefe & Huber Publishers

Differences Between "Normal" and "OCD" Obsessions

Researchers have found some important differences between "normal" obsessions and clinical (OCD) obsessions. In particular:

1. OCD obsessions are *more distressing* than normal obsessions,
2. OCD obsessions are *resisted more strongly* than are normal obsessions, and,
3. OCD obsessions are *more repetitive* than normal obsessions,

The rest of this handout will explain these differences so that you understand how the distressing (anxiety-provoking), recurring, and intense OCD obsessions develop from normal everyday intrusive thoughts (normal obsessions).

A. Why are OCD obsessions distressing?

Although everyone has unwanted distressing intrusive thoughts, it turns out that people have different ways of *interpreting* the meaning of these kinds of thoughts. When such thoughts are interpreted as especially threatening, it causes the thoughts to evoke fear, anxiety, and distress.

Let's look at how people with and without OCD interpret their intrusive unwanted thoughts. Research shows that people *without* OCD dismiss their intrusive unwanted thoughts as "mental noise". They recognize that such thoughts (even thoughts about disturbing things) are normal and meaningless. For example, a person without OCD who experiences a unwanted thought might say to him or herself, "that's a silly thought, I would never do that," or "that thought doesn't make any sense." When this happens, the person doesn't pay any more attention to the thought, and the thought soon passes without difficulty.

On the other hand, people with OCD tend to *misinterpret* these normal intrusive thoughts as very meaningful, significant, and threatening or dangerous. For example:

- "It is bad to have this kind of thought"
- "If I am thinking of something bad, it must be true"
- "If I think of something awful, it means I am an awful person"
- "If I have bad thoughts, it means I am losing my mind or that I will do something terrible"

When a person interprets his or her own thoughts as dangerous or threatening, this is what makes him or her feel distressed and anxious. After all, if you really believe that having certain unwanted thoughts means that something bad is about to happen, it would be normal to feel afraid. However, it is important to see that the real problem is the mistaken interpretation of the intrusive thought, not the thought itself. The thought is a normal experience. It is not actually harmful. *Misinterpreting normal intrusive thoughts as dangerous makes the thoughts become distressing.*

From: J.S. Abramowitz: *Obsessive-Compulsive Disorder*   Hogrefe & Huber Publishers

B. Why are OCD obsessions resisted?

Misinterpreting certain unwanted intrusive thoughts as dangerous leads not only to distress, but it also makes you want to resist or push the thought out of your mind. You can probably see how someone would try to resist an intrusive upsetting negative thought if they interpreted this thought to be significant, important, or dangerous.

C. Why are OCD obsessions repetitive?

People with OCD report that their intrusive obsessional thoughts are repetitive (they occur more frequently than do normal obsessions). Sometimes such thoughts are triggered by reminders in the environment, but at other times, they just seem to pop up from "out of the blue." The repetitiousness of obsessions also has a lot to do with how a person interprets these kinds of thoughts.

Specifically, once an intrusive thought is interpreted as threatening, it activates the body's automatic danger detection system (the "fight-flight" system) which causes the person to become hyper alert and "on guard" for the perceived threat. This is a normal and adaptive response whenever threat is perceived because it helps protect us from danger. For instance, if you had to walk across a busy street, your "fight or flight" response would kick in and you would become very aware of the cars coming toward you. You would scan the road for cars so that you could run out of the way to safety (*flight*) if you had to.

In the case of OCD obsessions, the perceived threat is an otherwise normal intrusive thought that has simply been *misinterpreted* as threatening. These misinterpretations lead people with OCD to become hyper-aware of (preoccupied with) their unwanted thoughts as if they were truly dangerous (which, as we have seen, is not at all the case). This natural tendency to become preoccupied with intrusive thoughts that are considered dangerous helps to explain the repetitiveness of obsessions in OCD.

There are other ways that people with OCD respond to their intrusive thoughts that can increase the repetitiveness of obsessions. For example, humans are not very good at controlling their thoughts. So, trying to push unwanted thoughts out of your head (called *thought suppression*) actually leads to an *increase* in the unwanted thought. This is a normal phenomenon—just see what happens if you try *not* to think of a pink elephant. If you have intrusive thoughts that you have misinterpreted as dangerous, leading you to try to force the thoughts out of your mind, you will probably end up with more of the bad thought (leading to a vicious cycle of more anxiety and futile attempts to suppress, and so on).

Conclusions

In conclusion, it is important to realize that everyone has intrusive, unwanted, upsetting thoughts from time to time. These thoughts are normal. They do not suggest any danger, evil, perversion, immorality, etc. They are simply senseless thoughts. The major difference between people with and without OCD is in how these kinds of thoughts are interpreted or appraised. People with OCD *misinterpret* these thoughts as significant, meaningful, and dangerous. This leads to anxiety and distress. It also makes the thoughts seem to take on a "life of their own." One aim of treatment for OCD is to help you learn how to properly regard these thoughts as "mental noise" so that they no longer cause obsessional problems.

Hogrefe & Huber Publishers

Cognitive Distortions in OCD

1. **Intolerance of Uncertainty:** Need for a 100% guarantee of safety (absolute certainty). Any hint of doubt or ambiguity is interpreted to mean a negative outcome is probable.

2. **Overestimation of Threat:** Exaggerating (a) the probability of negative outcomes, and/or (b) the seriousness of negative consequences.

3. **Overestimation of Responsibility:** Believing that one holds the power to prevent negative outcomes. Also, believing that the failure to prevent harm is the same as causing harm.

4. **Significance of Thoughts:** Believing that senseless, intrusive, and unwanted thoughts are important or very meaningful in one way or another.
   - **Moral Thought-Action Fusion:** Belief that thoughts are morally equivalent to behaviors.
   - **Likelihood Thought-Action Fusion:** Belief that thinking about something bad will lead to the corresponding action or event.

5. **Need to Control Thoughts:** Believing that one can and should control unwanted bad thoughts; and that they must do so to prevent negative outcomes.

6. **Intolerance of Anxiety:** Believing that anxiety or discomfort could persist forever or spiral out of control and lead to "going crazy," or other harmful consequences.

7. **The "Just Right" Error (Perfectionism):** The sense that things must be "just right," even, orderly, or perfect in order to feel comfortable.

8. **Emotional reasoning:** Assuming that danger is present based simply on the fact that you are feeling anxious ("If I feel anxious, there must be danger").

From: J.S. Abramowitz: *Obsessive-Compulsive Disorder*   Hogrefe & Huber Publishers

Fear Hierarchy Form

Situational Exposure Items	SUDS	Order
1.		
2.		
3.		
4.		
5.		
6.		
7.		
8.		
9.		
10.		
11.		
12.		
13.		
14.		
15.		
16.		
17.		
18.		
19.		
20.		
Imaginal Exposure Items	SUDS	Order
1.		
2.		
3.		
4.		
5.		
6.		
7.		
8.		

Hogrefe & Huber Publishers

The 10 Commandments for Successful Exposure

1. **Exposure practices should be planned and structured.** Prepare for the exercise in advance to make sure that it is conducted properly.

2. **Exposure practices should be repeated frequently.** Practice the same exposure tasks over and over until they become easier and provoke minimal distress.

3. **Do Exposure gradually.** Begin with exposure tasks that provoke only moderate levels of distress and work up to more difficult tasks.

4. **Expect to feel uncomfortable.** Exposure tasks must initially evoke discomfort to be successful. This discomfort is temporary and it will subside as you remain in the task and as you repeat the task.

5. **Don't fight the discomfort.** You will not benefit from exposure if you fight the anxiety (you might as well not do the task at all). Instead, just let yourself feel anxious. The worst thing that can happen is that you will temporarily feel uncomfortable.

6. **Don't use subtle avoidance strategies.** Complete exposure practices without using distraction, anti-anxiety medication, alcohol, and other such strategies.

7. **Use exposure practices to test negative predictions about the consequences of facing your fear.** Before starting the exposure, think about what you are afraid might happen during the task. Afterwards, review what you learned from the exposure and how it compares to your original fearful prediction. Did the worst possible thing happen? How did you manage?

8. **Keep track of your fear level.** Pay attention to how you are feeling during the exposure task. Take note of your anxiety level at regular intervals and rate your fear level from 0–100.

9. **Exposure should last until anxiety has significantly declined.** Continue the exposure until anxiety goes down by at least 40% to 50%.

10. **Practice exercises by yourself.** It is helpful to conduct some exposures by yourself because the presence of other people can sometimes make us feel artificially safe.

From: J.S. Abramowitz: *Obsessive-Compulsive Disorder*   Hogrefe & Huber Publishers

Exposure Practice Form

Name: _____ Date: _____ Time: _____

Session Number: _____

1. Description of the exposure exercise:

_____

_____

2. Feared outcome of exposure:

_____

_____

3. Estimated probability of the feared outcome (0–100%): _____ %

4. Estimated severity of the feared outcome (0–100%): _____ %

5. Every _____ minutes during the exposure, rate SUDS from 0 to 100:

- SUDS when beginning exposure (0–100) _____

SUDS	SUDS	SUDS	SUDS	SUDS
1. _____	7. _____	13. _____	19. _____	25. _____
2. _____	8. _____	14. _____	20. _____	26. _____
3. _____	9. _____	15. _____	21. _____	27. _____
4. _____	10. _____	16. _____	22. _____	28. _____
5. _____	11. _____	17. _____	23. _____	29. _____
6. _____	12. _____	18. _____	24. _____	30. _____

6. Describe the outcome of the exposure. What was learned?

_____

_____

7. Revised probability estimate: (0–100%): _____ %

8. Revised severity estimate: (0–100%): _____ %

Hogrefe & Huber Publishers

Bipolar Disorder

In the series: Advances in Psychotherapy – Evidence-Based Practice

Rober P. Reiser, Larry W. Thompson

The past 10 years have seen a dramatic increase of interest in psychosocial treatments of bipolar disorder. There is now substantial empirical evidence suggesting the effectiveness of such treatments. However, this accumulated information has not yet been transferred into clinical practice in many settings.

Help is now at hand. This compact volume brings to the practitioner a comprehensive, evidence-based approach to the treatment of bipolar disorder that is practical, easily accessible, and can be readily applied in clinical practice.

This practitioner's guide begins by describing the main features of bipolar disorder and considerations for differential diagnosis based on DSM-IV and ICD-10 criteria. Following this, current theories and models are described, along with decision trees for evaluating the best treatment options. The volume then guides the reader through a systematic, integrated approach to treatment, based on the best of recent research. The authors describe a structured directive therapy that is also collaborative and client centered. Special considerations, including managing suicide risk, substance misuse, and medication nonadherence, are addressed. The volume is rounded off by the inclusion of clinically oriented tools and sample forms.

Robert P. Reiser · Larry W. Thompson

Bipolar Disorder

Advances in
Psychotherapy
Evidence-Based Practice

HOGREFE

2005, 120 pages, softcover
ISBN: 0-88937-310-8 , US $ / € 24.95
Standing order price US $ / € 19.95
(minimum 4 successive vols.)
*Special rates for members of the Society of Clinical Psychology (APA D12) - Single volume: US $19.95
- Standing order: US $17.95 per volume
(please supply membership # when ordering)

Table of Contents

Order online at: **www.hhpub.com**

Heart Disease

In the series: Advances in Psychotherapy – Evidence-Based Practice

Judith A. Skala, Kenneth E. Freedland, Robert M. Carney

Despite the stunning progress in medical research that has been achieved over the past few decades, heart disease remains the leading cause of death and disability among adults in many industrialized countries. Behavioral and psychosocial factors play important roles in the development and progression of heart disease, as well as in how patients adapt to the challenges of living with this illness. This volume in the series *Advances in Psychotherapy* provides readers with a succinct introduction to behavioral and psychosocial treatment of the two most prevalent cardiac conditions, coronary heart disease and congestive heart failure. It summarizes the latest research on the intricate relationships between these conditions and psychosocial factors such as stress, depression, and anger, as well as behavioral factors such as physical inactivity and nonadherence to cardiac medication regimens. It draws upon lessons learned from a wide range of studies, including the landmark ENRICHD and SADHART clinical trials. It then goes on to provide practical, evidence-based recommendations and clinical tools for assessing and treating these problems. *Heart Disease* is an indispensable treatment manual for professionals who work with cardiac patients.

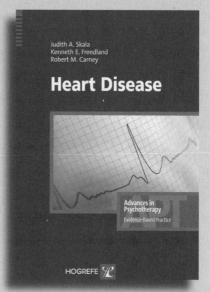

Judith A. Skala
Kenneth E. Freedland
Robert M. Carney

Heart Disease

Advances in
Psychotherapy
Evidence-Based Practice

HOGREFE

2005, 90 pages, softcover
ISBN: 0-88937-313-2 , US $ / € 24.95
Standing order price US $ / € 19.95
(minimum 4 successive vols.)
*Special rates for members of the Society of Clinical Psychology (APA D12) - Single volume: US $19.95
- Standing order: US $17.95 per volume
(please supply membership # when ordering)

Table of Contents

1. Description: Terminology • Definition • Epidemiology • Course and Prognosis • Differential Diagnosis • Comorbidities • Diagnostic Procedures and Documentation
2. Theories and Models of the Disorder
3. Diagnosis and Treatment Indications
4. Treatment: Methods of Treatment • Mechanisms of Action • Efficacy and Prognosis • Variations and Combinations of Methods • Problems in Carrying out the Treatments
5. Case Vignettes
6. Further Reading
7. References
8. Appendix: Tools and Resources

Order online at: **www.hhpub.com**

HOGREFE

Childhood Maltreatment

In the series: Advances in Psychotherapy – Evidence-Based Practice

Christine Wekerle, Alec L. Miller, David A. Wolfe, Carrie B. Spindel

The serious consequences of child abuse or maltreatment are among the most challenging things therapists encounter. There has in recent years been a surge of interest, and of both basic and clinical research, concerning early traumatization. This volume in the series *Advances in Psychotherapy* integrates results from the latest research showing the importance of early traumatization, into a compact and practical guide for practitioners. Advances in biological knowledge have highlighted the potential chronicity of effects of childhood maltreatment, demonstrating particular life challenges in managing emotions, forming and maintaining healthy relationships, healthy coping, and holding a positive outlook of oneself. Despite the resiliency of many maltreated children, adolescent and young adult well-being is often compromised. This text first overviews our current knowledge of the effects of childhood maltreatment on psychiatric and psychological health, then provides diagnostic guidance, and subsequently goes on to profile promising and effective evidence-based interventions. Consistent with the discussions of treatment, prevention programming that is multi-targeted at issues for maltreated individuals is highlighted. This text helps the practitioner or student to know what to look for, what questions need to be asked, how to handle the sensitive ethical implications, and what are promising avenues for effective coping.

2005, ca. 104 pages, softcover
ISBN: 0-88937-314-0 , US $ / € 24.95
Standing order price US $ / € 19.95
(minimum 4 successive vols.)
*Special rates for members of the Society of Clinical Psychology (APA D12) - Single volume: US $19.95
- Standing order: US $17.95 per volume
(please supply membership # when ordering)

Table of Contents

Order online at: **www.hhpub.com**

Problem and Pathological Gambling

In the series: Advances in Psychotherapy – Evidence-Based Practice

James P. Whelan, Andrew W. Meyers

Over the past 30 years there has been a dramatic increase in the availability of convenient and legal gambling opportunities. Most people can reach a casino in a matter of a few hours, lottery tickets in minutes, or an online gaming site in seconds. Accompanying this proliferation of gambling is a growing understanding that between 5% and 9% of adults experience significant to severe problems due to their gambling activities. These problems have become a real health concern, with substantial costs to individuals, families, and communities.

The objective of this book is to provide the clinician – or graduate student – with essential information about problem and pathological gambling. After placing this behavioral addiction and its co-occurring difficulties in perspective, by describing its proliferation, the associated costs, and diagnostic criteria and definitions, the authors present detailed information on a strategy to assess and treat gambling problems in an outpatient setting.

They go on to provide clear and easy-to-follow intervention guidelines, including homework assignments, for a brief and cost-efficient cognitive behavioral approach to problem gambling, involving stepped care and guided self-change. Means of countering problems and barriers to change and vivid case vignettes round off this thorough, but compact guide for clinicians.

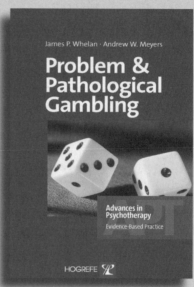

James P. Whelan · Andrew W. Meyers

Problem & Pathological Gambling

Advances in Psychotherapy
Evidence-Based Practice

HOGREFE

2005, ca. 104 pages, softcover
ISBN: 0-88937-312-4 , US $ / € 24.95
Standing order price US $ / € 19.95
(minimum 4 successive vols.)
*Special rates for members of the Society of Clinical Psychology (APA D12) - Single volume: US $19.95
- Standing order: US $17.95 per volume
(please supply membership # when ordering)

Table of Contents

1. Description: Terminology and Definitions • Epidemiology • Course and Prognosis • Differential Diagnosis • Comorbidities • Diagnostic Procedures and Documentation
2. Theories and Models of the Disorder
3. Diagnosis and Treatment Indications
4. Treatment: Methods of Treatment • Mechanisms of Action • Efficacy and Prognosis • Variations and Combinations of Methods • Problems and Barriers to Change
5. Case Vignette
6. Further Reading
7. References
8. Appendix: Tools and Resources

Order online at: **www.hhpub.com**

HOGREFE

Advances in Psychotherapy – Evidence-Based Practice

Developed and edited in consultation with the Society of Clinical Psychology (APA Division 12).

Pricing / Standing Order Terms

Regular Prices: Single-volume – $24.95; Series Standing Order – $19.95
APA D12 member prices: Single-volume – $19.95; Series Standing Order – $17.95
With a Series Standing Order you will automatically be sent each new volume upon its release. After a minimum of 4 successive volumes, the Series Standing Order can be cancelled at any time. If you wish to pay by credit card, we will hold the details on file but your card will only be charged when a new volume actually ships.

Order Form (please check a box)

[ ] I would like to place a Standing Order for the series at the special price of US $ / €19.95 per volume, starting with volume no. ....

[ ] I am a D12 Member and would like to place a Standing Order for the series at the special D12 Member Price of US $ / € 17.95 per volume, starting with volume no. ......
My APA D12 membership no. is:

[ ] I would like to order the following single volumes at the regular price of US $ / € 24.95 per volume.

[ ] I am a D12 Member and would like to order the following single volumes at the special D12 Member Price of US $ / € 19.95 per volume.
My APA D12 membership no. is:

Qty.	Author / Title / ISBN	Price	Total
		Subtotal	
	WA residents add 8.8% sales tax; Canadians 7% GST		
	Shipping & handling: USA – US $6.00 per volume (multiple copies: US $1.25 for each further copy) Canada – US $8.00 per volume (multiple copies: US $2.00 for each further copy) South America: – US $10.00 per volume (multiple copies: US $2.00 for each further copy) Europe: – € 6.00 per volume (multiple copies: € 1.25 for each further copy) Rest of the World: – € 8.00 per volume (multiple copies: € 1.50 for each further copy)		
		Total	

[ ] Check enclosed   [ ] Please bill me   [ ] Charge my: [ ] VISA   [ ] MC   [ ] AmEx

Card # _____ CVV2/CVC2/CID # _____ Exp date _____

Signature _____

Shipping address (please include phone & fax) _____

_____

_____

_____

Order online at: **www.hhpub.com**

Hogrefe & Huber Publishers • 30 Amberwood Parkway · Ashland, OH 44805 • Tel: (800) 228-3749 · Fax: (419) 281-6883
Hogrefe & Huber Publishers, Rohnsweg 25 • D-37085 Göttingen, Germany, Tel: +49 551 49609-0, Fax: +49 551 49609-88
E-Mail: custserv@hogrefe.com